The ethos of this bok is a joyful commual ent[...] [...] of energy, reflected in the rich tapetsry of Tapeley Park. My greatest thanks go to those who have contributed time, effort or ideas to bring this manuscript to fruition.

Thank you to all the individuals who have passed through on their life's journey, for however long. Without you the story would be far less entertaining.

For the colourful and unique artistic style of the illustrations, credit goes to Sue Sutherland and Moly Sutherland-O-Gara.

A special thanks goes to the dream team, artist Gea Austen and fellow author Nickie Joy, for keeping me grounded and the book on track. Lynton, my bud, for being there for me.

To Daphne and the labour of love we have created. I thank you from the bottom of my heart for all the hours of typing and retyping and for being my confidante.

Guy, my best friend, my inspration. Thank you for the years of companionship and shared thinking. You are a truly humble activitist who has done more for this planet than anyone will ever know, I salute you.

Printed and bound by Amazon

Find out more about the author and his commitment to sustainability, visit: www.tapeleydiaries.co.uk

ISBN: 9798363201264

This book is dedicated to

Daphne Lovelace

and

Gordon Steer

Contents:

Roger, Lord Crust & his band of merry "misfits"

Hector Christie

"It's not what you gain

but what you give

that denotes the worth

of

the live you live"

Hector Christie

Mr. Sniffy arrived at Crustington Manor one icy cold February morning. Mr. Sniffy, wearing a rainbow coloured hat, rainbow jumper, rainbow shirt and no shoes or socks- with piercings in every part of his body which could be pierced (including all 10 toes) wanted somewhere to live.

The portly Lord of the Manor, wearing shorts, smoking jacket and smart green hat to cover up his Homer Simpson-like head, opened the door. Lord 'Roger' Crust was immediately struck, and slightly impressed, by the gentleman's footwear (or lack of it) on the coldest day of winter so far. "You're not wearing shoes . . ."

"No, shoes are a form of corporate tax on walking . . ." Lord Crust, himself a fan of the alternative, unconventional and downright wacky, instantly fell in love with Mr. Sniffy. "Do you want somewhere to live?"

Lord Crust took Mr. Sniffy down to a courtyard which had a 'space' in one corner and was struck by the sudden, and seemingly random, machinelike bursts of sniffing fits that exuded from the lean, rather serious, gentleman at his side. On reaching the courtyard, Lord Crust started explaining the modus operandi of the community at Crustington Manor when something extraordinary and rather unexpected happened. . .

Midway through Lord Crust's most serious bit of dialect, a beaming smile appeared on Mr.Sniffy's face for the first time throwing Lord Crust off his stride. 'Why is Mr. Sniffy suddenly looking so happy?' thought Lord Crust with furrowed brow. Lord Crust, realising Mr. Sniffy was not listening to a word he was saying, looked Mr. Sniffy up and down where he noticed Mr. Sniffy's left foot moving back and forth on a freshly laid dog poo. 'No wonder Mr. Sniffy was smiling' thought the easily impressed Lord Crust who decided there and then that Mr. Sniffy was exactly what

Crustington Manor needed.

Mr. Sniffy was from the far left of the political spectrum and proclaimed to be "the only genuine anarchist in the country," a claim unabated and matched only by his deep respect and unconditional love for Margaret Thatcher. There was nothing Mr. Sniffy enjoyed more than putting the Socialists (and frequent visitors to Crustinigton Manor) firmly in their place.

Mr. Sniffy, aged 45 with 5 grandchildren – two of whom he'd actually met (albeit recently), had taken acid every day for 16 years and concluded that "acid had absolutely no negative effects or collateral damage on the brain whatsoever." Indeed, the first day after he kicked his habit, he did an A-level in Maths and got 94%, and the only reason he didn't get 100% was because "he didn't have time to finish the last question."

Mr. Sniffy, along with most of the other 25 or so inhabitants of Crustington, had come to the Manor on the back of the Didgeridoo Festivals. These were the 'Festivals of the land that time forgot'. The once Biannual event – which then briefly became 'Triannual' (a Christmas bash became essential for some who found the gap between September to the May Day event too much to bear) attracted the 'blanket-wearing-crusty-locks-protruding-through-holes-in-leather-hat brigade'. The large field in front of Crustington overlooking the ocean was like the Bean field at Stonehenge before the police moved in . . . beautiful traveller trucks, gypsy wagons, teepees and fires around which the many travellers (mostly musicians) sat and played music. Nobody left the site until every last spec of rubbish had been bagged up and sorted.

Mr.Sniffy, however, would start sorting out his skirts/sarongs, nail varnish and extra piercings weeks before each event. Such was his excitement he'd always peak on the Friday night, consuming vast quantities of the type of cocktail marine biologists would use to anaesthetise a blue whale.

Mr. Sniffy was an extremely conscientious worker. His military background meant he was never late and his time sheets summarised, to be fair, 'his work to the second'.

Mr. Sniffy's first port of call was working for Jennifer in the Permaculture garden. After a couple of weeks Jennifer, concerned by the regular visits of Health and Safety Officers, took 'Linas' to the farm shop to buy some 'work' boots. Jennifer had noticed an offer on steel-capped boots for £10 which would last forever.

Mr. Sniffy came out of the farm shop holding a pair of bright pink wellington boots which cost him £18 and lasted two weeks allowing him to revert to type.

Mr. Sniffy had never taken orders from a woman before and was most certainly not going to start now. As a matter of course he'd question, challenge (and often downright refuse) everything Jennifer asked him to do. After 2 months Jennifer sacked 'Linas' and sent him off to work with the 2 (understandably) grumpy old gardeners responsible for the Italian gardens, lawns, trees, lake and kitchen garden. The no questions matter of fact 'do what you're told' suited Mr. Sniffy and his army background.

The Permaculture at Crustington had been (until Jennifer eventually turned things around) a dumping ground for the lazy, work-shy, pot-smoking-hippy types . . . First there were the 'slug-relocating hippies'. This was when a motley looking crew of crusty ladies and gentleman had quickly ensconced themselves in caravans, 'outbuildings,' the house itself and The 'Pikey' site between 2000 and 2003.

Lord Crust, himself a product of the private school system and as such not as worldly wise as 'normal' people, was struck, even taken-aback, that many of the ladies had hairier legs (and of course armpits) than he.

Roger would occasionally take time out to marvel at the hippies at 'work'. He'd watch in quiet disbelief as the hippies gently rummaged through the vegetation of predominately perennial vegetables looking for slugs. On eventually finding a slug (they couldn't work too fast lest they accidentally tread on one of God's creatures), they'd gather round and say a few loving words of warning "now you mustn't be a naughty slug and sneak back in to this garden under cover of darkness or you'll be in trouble next time . . ." They'd then pop the slug in their bucket and carefully relocate the little fellow just over the fence. The process would be repeated the next day and the day after that – more often than not, no doubt, with the same cheeky slug.

'Iree' Mike was a South African with the longest Didgeridoo you'd ever seen (and the first person of many from the Didge Fests to move to Crustington). 'Iree' got together with Yvette, - a cute Romanian, slight of figure with a belief in all things 'natural'. They 'worked' (if that is the correct word) in the Permaculture garden wearing the bare minimum of cloth covering their respective nether regions, causing the proportion of male visitors to female to noticeably increase in that year.

'Iree', called as such because this is how he described everybody and every situation, only every lost his temper twice. The first time was on Exmoor where, with other members of the 'community,' he got lost looking for magic mushrooms when a thick mist descended. The second time was when he accompanied Lord Crust, with a few others, to a farmers' debate about GM (Genetically Modified) crops in Barnstaple. Roger was up against an elderly, wily, pinched-looking gentleman from 'Cropgen' - a company of impartial (supposedly) scientists, called Mr. 'Slime'.

Mr. Slime 'coincidentally' had nothing but good to say about GM

(it was discovered later that Cropgen was funded by the Biotec Industry). The well-oiled Mr. Slime got Lord Crust to lose his temper twice - which helped him win a unanimous vote with the farmers present (a profound lesson for Roger ensuring he never made the same mistake again). 'Iree' had asked Mr Slime about how much testing had been done to ascertain the safety (or otherwise) to humans of eating GM food "because if it had been independently tested for 10 years, I'd have no problem eating it." Mr. Slime ducked, dived and cleverly avoided giving a straight answer ('he's obviously been to politics training school' thought a beedy Roger) . . . "Just go to our website it's all on there" . . .

"That man there   . . .was extremely 'UnIREE'" an exceedingly angry Iree commented afterwards.

After 2 years it was time for Iree and his beloved to move on. Roger would miss the didge being played over supper to him, his children and community comrades by the beautiful blonde dreadlocked hippy sitting cross-legged by the sink (sometimes Iree would place the end of the didge in the sink to 'boost the resonance'). However, after a diet of raw food (collected and consumed randomly rather than scientifically in the nutritional sense) both Yvette and Iree had lost

every spare piece of body fat (not that there was much there anyway) and that part of the brain that encourages the body to 'work'.

As Iree was leaving, he noticed Roger's Rocket propelled Grenade (RPG) case next to the deep freeze . . . "Iree, Iree, Iree (said Iree) "could I possibly have that to house my didge for the plane journey? I've been looking everywhere for a 'didge holder'". Lord Crust immediately visualised Iree striding into Heathrow, this during a period of high alert from possible Al Qaida attacks, being surrounded by a fully armed SWAT team pointing at the poor hippy . . . "Everybody down on the ground . . ." with Mike yelling "all is ireeeee . . ." as he undid the case to reveal his beautiful didgeridoo. Sadly (for the scheming few) a community member saw Iree hitching on the A39, asked him where he was going, and pointed out the obvious.

If some from the aforesaid workforce could be bracketed in the U for 'ugh' league in terms of initiative and effort, there was plenty afoot to fill the remaining letters of the alphabet. There were also

WARNING
2.10
NO FESTIVAL CAN TRUST THIS PERSON

those with an unpleasant edge . . . "I don't ever work 'til the afternoon . . ." announced 'Matty' on arrival who, after he left pinning poor Roger to the wall, Crustington received a "Festival Parasite warning" circulated to every person doing festivals . . . "Big chip on shoulder, short fuse, once he gets into 'hard done by' you get the nasty side: tyres slashed, fuel tanks filled with dirt blah blah." This accompanied by a pic of the sneering 'Matty' himself.

In the level below (the lowest of the lot) there were those who worked quite hard, said all the right things to win Roger's trust then shafted him in the back and did (literally) anything to take control (class A drugs would help enormously in maintaining this delusional state of mind.) Heading this 'gruesome' category was the charming and handsome Adrian Jones.

Adrian had a number of girlfriends (and boyfriends) none more 'lovely' than Sam - a 'lady' of Afro-American descent and the cunning of a dog fox in its prime. Together they orchestrated one of two 'takeover bids' to oust the genial and largely good willed Lord Crust.

Nothing was beyond the boundaries for these two dirty rotten scoundrels. The 'butter wouldn't melt' was the umbrella used to get others to do no work/the bare minimum (not that they needed much encouragement with the amount of ganja they were consuming). They would then project the tried and tested 'hard done by vibe' and blame Roger for everything that was wrong in their lives. 12 hours a week for those living in caravans, outbuildings and trucks with free electricity, no water rates or Council tax plus free organic veg; and 14 hours for the equivalent inside the house, was deemed a ruthless exploitation of the proletariat.

Such was the feeling of grievance, jealousy and bitterness – vandalism, theft and pointless acts of vengeance were rife. 'A professional psychologist's dream' some might say, but with his favourite tractor vandalised at busy times, the gates to the pigs and Highland cattle being regularly opened, and young boisterous 'guests' living in Roger's house even picking fights with him, 'it weren't no bed of roses' as the saying goes . . . Indeed, one fine day a professional psychologist DID move into the grounds, just like the Big Bad Wolf DID move into the wood where Peter lived . . .

To quell the noisy rage and satisfy the 1 or 2 who were actually working, Roger had to somehow find a type of 'work' that 'Keith' could do if he were to avoid being left solely with the dregs. One useful sleepless night he got the answer.

In the spring of 2003, one of Roger's Highland cows 'Mad Mel' (a name she didn't come to acquire lightly due to her aggressive loathing of all things human – especially Roger) had a calf. Getting newly born calves away from their mothers to ear tag and castrate (where appropriate) them in Rogers' matchstick-like 'corral' was often a matter of life or death. If Roger were to avoid a severe goring or worse, it was vital to have a sober hippy on hand to open and close the gate once Roger had grabbed the calf.

As you might have gleaned, a 'sober hippy' was hard to find at this time, but with a vet telling Roger that "Highlands' kill more farmers each year than the rest of the breeds put together" and the calf in question was Mad Mel's offspring, the man or woman on the gate was paramount. This was when Roger would grab the back leg of the bucking calf once the Mum was looking the other way – in order to ear tag and castrate (where necessary). It was around this time a 'cow was born . . .'

'Harold' was your text book, Walt Disney, fluffy, butter wouldn't melt, pretty calf – every child's dream animal to snuggle up to at night. It was the first time since Roger had acquired the cattle that one had been born from a Mum with no milk. Having farmed a largish flock of sheep for years (something he said he never enjoyed much "because of their inherent desire to kill themselves in every imaginative and/or stupid way possible from the time they are born") he knew the calf would need colostrum in the first 24 hours if it were to survive and be healthy. (Colostrum is rich thick milk full of antibodies to give immunity to disease. The only time it is produced is in the first 24 hours after giving birth, after which they produce milk).

'Keith', from South Africa, loved animals. He also professed to be a professional Ventriloquist and, with 'Joe Joe' on his right hand, did everything from open supermarkets in South Africa to entertaining ANC members. The lewdness of Joe Joe's mind aside, which at times beggared belief as to how Keith had avoided prison in most countries in which he had performed, the Ventriloquists' mouth moved as much (and at times perceptibly more) when Joe Joe was speaking as when Keith himself was. Keith saw in Harold what he saw in Joe Joe and, as such, wholeheartedly took on the role of Harold's 'surrogate father'. Keith, at last, had a 'job' . . . Everywhere Keith went, the fluffy calf bounded along too. Harold was to be found in Keith's abode – a ramshackle old cattle shed with the old medieval hayracks still in place, more often than not.

It was only because of Keith's inability to 'house train' Harold that he didn't live in the old cattle shed permanently.

Harold, however, did go to all the parties – except for those in the house itself. He was the life and soul of said 'soirees' until he (and his horns) reached a size which, combined with an increasingly boisterous and excitable nature, meant the odd minor injury inflicted upon the drunken revellers increased in frequency and severity.

The 'work' Keith was putting into Harold's formative months was still not enough to satisfy certain members of the community. The drums (or in this case 'Didgeridoos') of discontent with regard to Keith even amongst those who were perilously close to not being able to push a wheelbarrow – let alone re-locate a slug- was escalating.

Aside from a few fluffy bunnies and guinea pigs in 'Pets Corner,' Roger had taken on two New Zealand Kunne Kunne pigs. They were donated from a local kindergarten where the children had taught said pigs to sit on their haunches, raise a left trotter in the air, open their mouths and 'beg'.

During one of many frustrating sleepless nights as Roger worried himself sick as to how he was going to keep his flagging commune going, he had a 'Eureka' moment – (well . . .that's what he thought at the time): 'A daily Highland bull and Pig Show for the public. . .' Keith leapt at the idea of being let loose with the visitors – little did Roger know the risk he was taking.

At midday . . .ish, Keith would lead Harold into the pig field. Here he'd run from Harold and then feign injury causing Harold to try to lift Keith up with his small budding horns amongst a lot of kissing and cuddling. Keith would then pontificate whatever came into his (normally warped) mind. For example, the story of Moses and the Golden calf on Mount Sinai and how Harold was the direct descendent of said calf and as such was destined to become a beacon to Christians in the same way Hindus worship their cows. He'd then follow this up with the 'Pig and Peacock Show' . . .

Keith had somehow trained the 2 male peacocks roaming (posing) at will around the gardens to come at his call . . . "A warning to the ladies in the audience" he would say, with a knowing glint in his eye, "do not look at the 'eyes' in the peacocks' tail lest it give you 'sensations.'" "What sort of sensations sir?" a lady would inevitably ask whilst obediently averting her eyes as the peacocks arrogantly unfolded their voluptuous tails.

This would open the way to Keith having a conversation about his favourite subject for as long as folk chose to hang around.

As the shroud of darkness surrounding Crustington's ventriloquist in residence intensified, Keith had to be helped on his way if a total collapse was to be averted. No sooner than he left than (another) very tall, thin, bare footed gentleman with long grey hair 'manifested from the ether'.

'Wavey-Davey' (as Dave became known) had walked from John O' Groats to North Devon- barefoot. He had somehow heard about Crustington and (no doubt) the genial, accommodating nature of Roger. True to form, Lord Crust took pity on the exhausted looking gentleman before him and popped him into the place formerly known as 'Keith's space'.

Wavey-Davey was a product (victim) of the '60's and incredibly strong. 'Strawbale Ru', as he quickly became known, was starting to build the strawbale house at the time and needed some large chunks of granite to be transported up a steep hill to help make a spectacular entrance. Wavey-Davey spent each and every night carrying the massive lumps the 300 plus metres up the hill – the 'Aceeeeeed' creating 'Obelix' as his alter-ego in his sweet but befuddled mind. In the day he'd pace round and round in circles – even when Roger took him to the beach, causing families to pick up their picnics and children and move to a 'safer' place.

Whether it was the fact he was 'doing all the work where others were doing nothing', to 'pacing' or 'Father Time catching up with him', he resorted in his spare moments to 'purposefully' pacing around his space, cursing and threatening the world and the idle hippies. Those living nearby were scared witless and dear Wavey-Davey had to be 'moved on his merry way'.

There were, at this time, the odd individual who raised the Hippy bar to legendary status. Tristan was one such individual. One sunny morning there was a knock on Roger's door. On opening the door, Roger was met by 'Goth', all in black (as Goths are), with a nose protruding through a mop of black hair – the only clue that the effigy before him was indeed human. 'Is this Neil from the Young Ones or a character from the Furry Freak Brothers?' thought Lord

Crust.

Tristan knew someone who knew someone (etc) who lived at Crustington. That was good enough for Roger and, intrigued, he invited the 'spectre' inside for a cup of tea - the first of many as Roger would soon find out.

When Tristan pulled back his hair, which he only did to sip a cup of tea or draw deeply on the freshly made Bifta, he revealed skin with the pure whiteness of a newly made porcelain plate.

Tristan only once removed his shirt. It was during a hot summer's day down the coast at 'Welcome' beach where Lord Crust would sometimes take the hippies for a paddle or a surf.

Strawbale Ru was dumbstruck . . . "Tristan, you have the most beautiful curves of any man or woman I have ever seen". Indeed with his broad shoulders and hips with a very narrow waistline in between, Roger had to agree with Ru. Poor Tristan . . . he wasn't going to allow himself a tan that year.

Tristan easily slipped into the 'work' ethic at Crustington. He would venture out of his bedroom at 3pm for a few cups of tea in the kitchen. Full of the joys of spring, and having put a kettle on, he'd exclaim "anybody like a cup of Teeeeee?".

Following a 2-hour breakfast of cups of tea and spliffs, Tristan would go off to do the first of his 2 daily jobs. With the bucket of leftover food, he'd set off up a gentle slope to feed the pigs. The squeals of anticipation from Jarrick and 'Anneke' (Roger had a dubious habit of naming a pig after his latest girlfriend) were louder than usual, being they were not used to being fed so late in the day. The problem was Lord Crust loved Tristan, and couldn't find anything else Tristan could do.

Having fed the pigs (Tristan would stay as long as it took and only leave once every morsel of food had been consumed – which could take an hour), Tristan would then set off all the way to the other side of the grounds. In the wild lands next to the permaculture garden, the chickens needed to be put away before nightfall (Roger would always let them out in the mornings of course). Here Tristan would coax the chickens into their hut with a mixture of grain, copious amounts of love, and a few gentle words of warning about the 'big bad fox'.

One dark 'dark' night, the Crustington crew were all out in Barnstaple listening to a band. At midnight Tristan did the impossible. He went 'whiter than white' . . . "Oh heavy heavy . . .heavy heavy" he kept saying (yes, he was 'Neil' from the 'Young Ones' as we'd thought) . . . "I forgot to shut the chickens in . . ." We did all we could to reassure the highly stressed hippy that we were sure they'd be Ok for one night.

The next morning Roger's children went out to play. On the lawn next to the wild garden they found 3 dead chickens. In the wild garden itself they found another 8 dead. The one survivor had found a way through the fence to the permaculture garden where it spent the rest of its natural life before passing away peacefully in old age.

No-one had the heart to tell Tristan. No-one was in or near the kitchen at 3pm. Everybody heard the delirious wails emanating from the poor utterly distraught hippy, and everybody also knew no words of consolation would ease his devastation. At 3am Tristan packed his bags and left Crustington, and those who lived there, a less happy place than it had been.

Some months later news filtered back as to the whereabouts of Tristan and what he was up to. Tristan had managed to get a live-in job at a takeaway Pizzeria in Falmouth. He had acquired the job on the back of his expertise with computers. Tristan was selling (and delivering) Pizzas via internet orders.

Now most people, if they want a pizza, go to the pizzeria itself or ring up for a takeaway. Tristan would receive one order a week at midnight from a bunch of 'stoners' who lived half an hour away at Mevagissy. He would load up his van with the order and stay with said like-minded stoners until at least Tuesday before returning to 'work'. Tristan held the job down for an incredible 4 months - a feat that could only be put down to his devastating charm.

Over this period, the 'permaculture' garden naturally became the dumping ground for the main gardeners- Alan and Chris - who were responsible for maintaining the Italian terraces, walled kitchen garden, lake and Labyrinth. Without this option these professional gardeners would certainly have moved on and Lord Crust would have been left 'up the creek without a paddle' so to speak.

In a similar vein, his Lordship didn't quite realise what a jewel he had in Jennifer: dealing with issues of her 'workforce'; taking a frog to the vet after it had been spiked by a fork; calling out the RSPCA after finding a mouse nest in the compost heap; refusing to burn wood because there were woodlice in it; insisting on having a "Vegan Bonfire . . .?" and playing the flute to help the sunflowers grow larger as part of their 'working' hours, were a fundamental part of Jennifer's working day.

This, Lord Crust found out some years later, was the tip of the iceberg. Jennifer was a highly qualified gardener, who'd worked in the Physic Garden in London where she also had her own garden design and hands-on business. She was attracted to Crustington because, like an ever-increasing number of others, she was drawn to a more sustainable chemical-free approach to gardening.

The icing on the cake was Lord Crust giving her the option to move into the finally completed strawbale house - a house originally earmarked for his Lordship's right-hand man, and best friend, Leopold. That idea, though, was quickly scuppered by Leo's beloved, but determined, daughter Gaia, then aged 6, who took her stance due to her worst nightmare of the Big Bad wolf coming out of the forest and "huffing and puffing and blowing the house down". Thus, the way was paved for Jenny.

Folks from all walks of life, nationalities and backgrounds arrived at the Manor over this period. There was the 'naked' Frenchman Yvonne, and his equally naked belly dancing girlfriend; a pretty, but also naked, Belgian lady; buxom Hungarians, Australians, Canadians and . . . Germans (the first 'wave' as it turned out). 'Gerhard' rocked up the drive one spring morning in a beautiful tastily painted wooden truck. Lord Crust was having a lot of trouble with 'revolting hippies' at the time and was loathe to take on anymore potential trouble. However, bowled over by the German charm - Gerhard apologised profoundly to Lord Crust "for zi German football team knocking out zi England football team, zis ven zi English football team ver zi better side . . ." Roger agreed to him having a 2-week trial. The back car park was full of caravans and trucks, as was the 'pikey site', so Gerhard was given a pitch by himself (which turned out to be a good thing) by the old saw mill.

Gerhard 'knew his onions' so to speak and, in the only way the Germans do, determinedly set out to do as much "verk as all zi other hippies did put together." Lord Crust was chuffed he'd at last got something right (or so he thought) and gave himself a metaphorical pat on the back.

Within a short period, rumours started to abound (which always happened when things seemingly started to go well).

Alan and Chris - the long-suffering, understandably grumpy, proper gardeners- sent Gerhard down to the dumping ground for the lazy, work shy, slug relocating (and now psychopathic) types. Roger heard, on the (rampant) Tapeley grapevine, that Gerhard had picked a fight with 'Fae' (not the name she was christened with as was the case with so many - the name 'Debra' falling well short for consideration on the 'Crust/credibility scale') because she "vos not sticking to zi principles of Permaculture". Exasperated and let down yet again, Roger felt he might have to (reluctantly as always) pull his seemingly (to everybody else) inexhaustible diplomatic card for the umpteenth time.

Later that evening, whilst off to feed his Black Berkshire pigs, Lord Crust nearly jumped out of his skin when he heard a voice behind him yell "How can you allow zis field to get into such a disgusting state? It lets zi whole manor down and zi public will be appalled and not come back . . ." Roger tried, but failed, to explain that pigs 'rootle' - before gently helping him on his way.

For 10 years Crustington's 'Health and Harmony' Festivals dominated the summer scene. Roger acquired a huge 'cheap' (£1,500) marquee in 2000. The heavily stained (hence price) but solid marquee hosted its first H & H weekend that July. Vivian Dolby partnered Roger and they organised a whole gaggle of stall holders selling fluffy trinkets and crystals/shiny stones. These were mostly picked up by Roger's young daughter who, with the £20 pocket money she received (plus what she could blag), set the precedent of keeping the (semi) precious stone dealers in business for the next ten years.

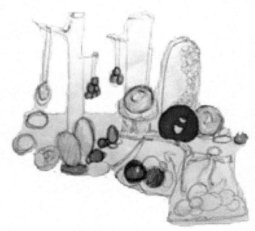

There were Didgeridoo makers/musicians a plenty, hoola-hoopers, belly dancers (which compromised 2 spirited blind ladies grinning from ear to ear), story tellers, reflexologists and 'healers' of all shapes and sizes all with a wide range of 'mystical' leanings/backgrounds; endless drumming and pipe circles, Tibetan bowl 'therapy' in the barn giving chakra healing on similar principles to receiving beneficial enlightenment in a 'Didge Tunnel'. Yes . . . you name it and Crustington did it - and all of this overlooking the Torridge Estuary across to Crow Point with the magical Lundy Island in the distance.

One beautiful summer's day at the last of the 4 Health and Harmony weekends in August 2001; 'Jesus' arrived at Crustington. Roger looked on in awe as the long brown haired fully 'enlightened one' glided and danced round the crystal healers, reflexologists and the spiritually attuned in the marquee raising the vibrations to nothing he'd seen before – even during the New Age phase a la David Icke orientation in the early 90's.

At this time Roger was licking his wounds having spent the previous 8 months fighting the corporate bandwagon attempting to eradicate the small, independent farmer using the guise of 'Foot and Mouth'. Roger had become radicalised with regular arrests and eventual imprisonment but along the way had made a lot of friends with those on the left side of left. One seemingly 'Icke went off his bike' such person was Noreena Hurtz, an anti-capitalist with whom Roger had recently gone to Italy on 'holiday' (well . . .the G8 summit in Genoa and most violent protests in Europe for 20 years). Noreena had come down to speak about important global issues and when Roger summoned up the nerve to invite Jeremy to the seminar the reply, lovingly delivered as it was, came back . . . "Yours is the path of the warrior and fear, mine that of the Enlightened One . . ." 'My God . . .this was the reincarnation of Jesus —no question' Roger thought as he somewhat shamefully slunk off to hear what Noreena had to say.

Lord Crust thought he had 'blown it' with this celestial being and doubted if he'd ever have another such opportunity. . .

Sometime the following year there was a knock on the door and there before him stood . . .Jeremy.

The resplendent all white regalia had given way to, for want of a better word, a more gracious even, dare Roger even 'think' it, 'normal' look. 'God he's really not that different from me' (Roger found himself guiltily thinking – before forcibly eradicating such ego orientated nonsense from his mind).

The ridiculous 'guilt' Lord Crust felt about inheriting so much when so many have so little meant Jeremy was given a space to rest his weary head – no references required from previous Landlords, no deposit, no trial period and (as some might feel) no clue. Jeremy was closely followed by his then 'partner' Sally-Anne.

Sally-Anne was a throwback to the hippy 60's. The first thing she did, unbeknown to anyone – particularly the gardeners- was to scatter 'seed' in the Tea Room border and all 3 borders on the Italian Terrace. 2-3 months later Tapeley's borders erupted in a 'dazzling' Chelsea Flower Show-esque carpet of multi-coloured pansies. The Head gardener had to put up with a lot of lazy, workshy types who simply wanted a free place to live, help themselves to whatever fruit and veg there was growing in the garden, and smoke weed whilst plying themselves with magic mushrooms (carpet bombed throughout the surrounding fields) between August and December. That said, to Alan and Chris, this was the straw that broke the camel's back.

Roger was by then now so wrapped up in his anti-capitalist fever- whether in London with trusted best friend Guy Taylor, going to G8 summits or heckling Prime Ministers Tony Blair and Gordon Brown etc- 'pansies in the borders' were low down on his 'to do list'. Indeed, Roger was on his very last legs when it came to the lazy, workshy, pot smoking 'manipulative' numpties he'd inadvertently surrounded himself with when . . . up stepped Leopold . . .

Roger first met Leopold on the picket lines at the Deep Moor pit in Torrington at the height of Foot and Mouth in 2001. Here protesters were picketing against the illegal dumping of healthy animals - brutally murdered - this so the (1%) could get their 'export' (of live animals packed tightly into crates across the channel and then lorries across Europe) licences back quickly. (The export licence was re-opened 3 months after the last slaughter or 2 years after the last vaccination - of which there was enough vaccine in store to do every animal in the UK at nearly 99% efficiency according to a 'leaked' document Roger received from MAFF - the despicable corporate-driven 'arm' of Blair's Government).

Leopold was sitting on the ground at the gates with others blocking 6 or so lorries full of mindlessly killed carcasses wearing a Brighton and Hove Albion shirt. Roger was brought up a passionate Brighton fan in the good old days of football hooliganism in the 70's. "Seagulls" . . . Roger chanted and was met by the same 'riposte' from his instantly new best friend.

Soon after this encounter, Leopold arrived at Crustington Manor. Having quickly weighed up the situation - folk of all denominations dumping their problems/issues on Roger's worn out *shoulders, Leopold offered to manage the place. It was an offer Roger instantly grabbed with both hands freeing him to get more stuck into attacking the Genetic Modification (and accompanying increase in devastating toxic pesticides - Roundup, 2-4D/Agent Orange, atrazine and the rest) in our food.*

Vodka is the Mouton Rothschild of spirits for most 'true' drinkers. The reason . . . it doesn't smell. Like most seasoned, (hardened)drinkers, not telling the truth becomes as easy as, well . . . having another vodka. The odd time Roger did catch his 'right hand man' pouring the clear liquid from a hip flask into an aspartame (i.e. highly carcinogenic) rich glass of Diet Coke (always under the table), Leopold 'adeptly' brushed it off in a "don't worry . . .this is to celebrate a special day/demo/pretty much anything and is the first I've had for months" kind of way . . . .

To be fair to Leopold, his heart was very much in the right place allowing Roger to step back a bit. BUT . . . a spectacularly raging 'drinker' organising work schedules, AND implementing them, for 25+ hippies; a 'bed of roses' it was NOT going to be . . .

The food produced to feed both the Tea Rooms and those living at the Manor from the kitchen garden and Permaculture was not enough. It was Leopold's idea to create a space for those living at 'Il Crust' to have their own allotments. The space set aside was below where Roger kept his Kune Kune pigs.

A couple of years after Leopold left, Roger visited a pub in Northam with his football mates (Roger had been an above average - his words of course- semi-professional footballer for the previous 15 or so years). Following their 2nd or 3rd pint, 'James' (the pub Landlord and old friend of Roger's) spoke about a barman he recently had to sack . . . "A few months ago, this guy turned up in response to an advert for a new Manager. He was well turned out, articulate and 'practically' over qualified in many ways to run a pub". James thought he'd struck gold and could thereby spend more time on the golf course . . . Following a couple of months of stocktaking records, successful as the pub was, James noticed from the figures - especially those involving vodka, that the profits had taken a significant downturn . . .

"So what I did was to record who was on what shift then put small marks on the vodka bottles and was 'amazed' at how much that guy could put away . . ." "This person, by any chance, wasn't called Leopold was he . . .?" "Yes . . .do you know him . . .?" "Er, yes ...very well."

A few years later it was Roger's turn . . . Following a successful Demo, Football match (or practically anything, to be frank) it was down to the boozer for a what he thought a well-earned pint or 10. Caesars Palace Bideford was where 'everybody' ended up after 2am. It was also the venue where Roger honed his

après 2am party piece - crowd surfing (cut short when the 'crowd' thought it funny to step aside resulting in Roger being banned from the Palace where all he had to show for his endeavours was a deep cut on his chin, a damaged collar bone and a black eye).

A year or 2 after aforesaid 'party piece' Roger fell for the stunning Lucinda. Lucinda was a fair bit younger than Roger, very petit and a little coy (the sort of combination that sent Roger crazy). Roger heard about a Punk Rock concert comprising The Damned, The Jam, and the Stranglers.

With things not going to plan at all at the 'concert', Roger knew he had to pull a 'rabbit out of the hat' if he was to give himself any sort of chance whatsoever. With nothing to lose, Roger went to the top of the 'steep' hill above the baying masses and yelled . . . "I'm cummin' through". Thankfully this time the Red Sea didn't part and Roger got carted down at speed by the punk rockers and hurled over the security fence in front of the bands where he got a good spanking form 'security' before being chucked out of the concert, and, having been separated from his 'wannabe' girlfriend, embarked on the 10 mile walk home.

'Oh well . . . . .one did one's best' mused Roger.

2 days later, just as

Roger was metaphorically putting his latest failure into the 'put it down to experience' drawer, Roger received a phone call . . .

Unbeknown to Roger, his alcoholic intake had insidiously escalated to, what most would consider, 'severe danger levels'. Roger had his alcoholism 'reasonably' under control when he was playing for local semi-pro football clubs like Bideford, Barnstaple and Appledore. This in as much he wouldn't drink during the 2 days leading up to a match.

Once this discipline (of sorts) was no longer in place he allowed all discipline to go by the wayside. Roger never drank during the day but once the 'yard arm' hit 6pm he'd knock back a bottle of white wine within 20 minutes and simply carry on until he went to bed.

Roger's problem was first noticed by his friends at the 'Green Gathering' at Chepstow racecourse where he did a 'talk' each year. Having delivered his talk about his bug bear – Genetically Modified food– Roger would guzzle a cocktail of alcohol enough to get a whale sozzled where someone would find him in a bush next day.

Friends became concerned and many had words to say. Roger's family – especially his beautiful daughter and Mum– became so exasperated and let him know in no uncertain terms as he forgot appointments, lunch dates with his Mum (the worst) etc. Roger's troubles escalated when he became an active member of the 'say No to G.M.O' (genetically modified food) campaign– this following closely on the coattails of the wonderful Globalise Resistance, with best mate Guy Taylor at the helm.

'Seasoned' community inhabitants, Tamara and her long haired dreadlocked 'partner' Hazel moved in around that time. Yes, like so many of the 'travelling' community Hazel was born into a fairly well-off family before rebelling (understandable in many ways . . .) They were accompanied by their son Otaheites, a boy who was permanently naked, even in winter.

Roger had met Tamara a few months earlier at the G8 – Gleneagles and had been impressed by her passion. However, what the naive Roger hadn't catered for was that a hard-core extreme protester could potentially cause fairly hefty waves in a precarious, delicate community situation . . .

The volatile Tamara had been at the manor for 1 week when she demanded Roger give the community members an allotment each for which she would take full charge . . .Without a second thought Roger immediately said 'yes' and knew he'd guaranteed himself a highly valued 4 – 6 hours of peace and quiet when he wouldn't be put on the spot.

Positioned slap bang in the middle of the allotments 'Tammy' felt it her 'job' to dictate to those either side as to how folk should be managing their respective sites (by then re-named the 'Gaza Strip'). Fights (amazingly) didn't break out but the ensuing animosity and bad feeling way outweighed a 'decent bed of carrots' in poor old Roger's mind – who, as usual, was caught up pig-in-the-middle getting bashed every which way. (Roger tried this 'principle' once more when he gave up a quarter of the walled kitchen garden to locals . . . the result – as 'usual' . . . was phenomenal animosity between gardeners working hard with good yields and those 'too posh to weed' allowing weeds to 'seed' all over their neighbours' plots.)

EVERY CLOUD HAS A SILVER LINING (as the old saying goes) . . .

Tamara and her lovely partner Hazel had some very interesting friends who were part of a travelling theatre group and keen, after seeing photos of the 'lake', to do 3 consecutive nights of theatre – with 3 shows per night of between 15 to 30 people per show. . .

2 months later a 'circus' of travellers' trucks of varying colours arrived at the manor courtesy of a recommendation by Tamara. A young, vibrant group of 70+ people emerged and set up what could only be described as a 'Travellers' Village' underneath the relatively young Monteray Pine trees between the straw bale house and the pigs.

Wires and all sorts of gizmos were erected around the lake and, excitedly, Roger contacted his close friend James – a presenter and editor on West Country TV who covered most of Roger's distressing protests during Foot and Mouth. 'James' was intrigued and focussed his filming on a group of nymphs covered in mud and (to a lesser extent) strategically positioned leaves, scurrying around in the undergrowth. Unfortunately, Roger was informed, too many breasts had popped out during filming which meant it couldn't be 'aired/promoted' on the telly. But . . .no matter, the 'spectacle' was phenomenal . . .

As you walked down the path to the lake, a light lit up and from a branch of one of the highest oak trees a 'fairy' descended. With a sparkly flowing dress, white dreadlocks, and a twinkle in her eye the fairy announced that "we are now entering the world of 'magic and mysticism' . . . leave all Earthly thoughts behind . . . out of sight is out of mind . . ." Then following a 5-minute gawp (for the gentleman) of the semi- 'bare' ladies painted all shades of green, folk were led round the lake. The towering Thuja Plicata trees, Cedars, Scott's Pines and Oaks - many over 500 years old were, of course, an uplifting bonus.

Next stop was a beautiful blonde harpist resonating out chords of nectar summoning up the spirits of King Arthur, Lancelot and, of course, Merlin - this to 'awaken' the 'Lady of the Lake.'

As the group approached Roger's 'second' favourite tree . . .where a branch hangs loosely over to the island in the middle of the lake, a brightly lit-up sword broke the surface. The girl, who had been underwater for the previous 20 minutes, then sang a beautiful ballad - accompanied by the harpist (before disappearing back into the darkness of the cold murky water).

From here the group continued round the lake past the smaller 'feeder' ponds, BUT instead of carrying on back up the way they came down, the group were led along the eerily lit bottom track with fake cobwebs sporadically brushing against folk's cheeks. It was then the group were spun a story about approaching the 'lair of the Giant Spider' when all of a sudden, the group were faced with a giant spider's web spanning the path and up into the trees making the children (and some adults) go very quiet.

Our wizard/guide then quietly said . . ."Look behind you . . ." Screams broke out from all the children, and many of the adults, at the sight of a guy on 4 massive stilts standing 25 foot high with flashing red eyes closing in on the group thus forcing the (not so) merry throng into (and through)the giant web before them, with terrified children scrambling for their lives through the gaps in the web.

It was from there onward/deeper into the forest when the group encountered a large, well lit-up multi-coloured teepee just off the boggy path. Suddenly the door flap burst open and out popped a beaming modern-day Beatrix Potter like character wrapped up in smelly blankets with dreadlocks seemingly covering his whole anatomy . . .

"Come hither brave children . . .thou hast made it thus far

through dangers a plenty - now enter my home where I will give you the secrets of the forest . . ." 'Hazel' then took the children, and adults alike, and demonstratively and with full gusto - eyes popping out excitedly through thick brown facial hair, he came out with . . .well . . . the first thing that entered his head thus rounding up the deliciously dotty yet charming experience.

The lake, indeed, played a major role in all manner of ways . . . Hills and Harry rocked up one spring morning (unannounced as was the norm back then) and pitched in the back car park next to the polytunnels. Both had got firsts at Cambridge University after which they took one look at the world, dropped out and invested everything into what was to become their 'home.'

The multi coloured (ultimate) hippy truck was also home to the largest array of medicinal herbs all lined up on perfectly made wooden racks - shelf after shelf. They truly had a herb for every imaginable illness and were only too willing to 'treat' anybody and everybody. Harry was 'quiet' in the way 'Hills' was large and loud. Hills immediately took on the role of Mother Hen at Crustington with her 'ducklings' flocking in 2 by 2 - a true modern-day Noah's Ark.

It wasn't long before Hills and Harry announced their engagement. The 'Year and a Day' hand fasting (the favoured 'wedding' of the residents of the Crust) was to take place on the bottom terrace on Midsummer's day surrounded by the borders with the red brick house towering above the lot. The 150-odd (in more ways than could possibly be conceived) multi coloured attendees

were 'collected' (by Hills) from all corners of the UK (akin to the 'Child Catcher' in Chitty Chitty Bang Bang) where they formed a large circle where the newlyweds exchanged wreaths and medicinal herbs before an 'ohming' congregation.

The only interruption was when Tommy – a 16-year-old, (slightly) lose cannon who lived in the house with Roger, turned up wearing a rather crude phallic blow-up pink thing on his head holding a whirring chainsaw. By then practically anything was normal and no one batted an eyelid. (Tommy had been at Crustington since Foot and Mouth and had, days before, cut off 'Joe Joe's hand for being too pervy and creepy. This was when, long overdue, Keith was finally escorted down the drive with strict instructions never to return.)

It was then off to the lake for the hand fasting party of parties.

The décor was in a similar style to a party that had taken place there a few weeks earlier when the Glastonbury Rabbit Hole hard core had erected 20 odd 'themed' tents with the Mad Cows performing a 12-14 hour marathon set (well . . . that was slightly because nobody else could get a look in).

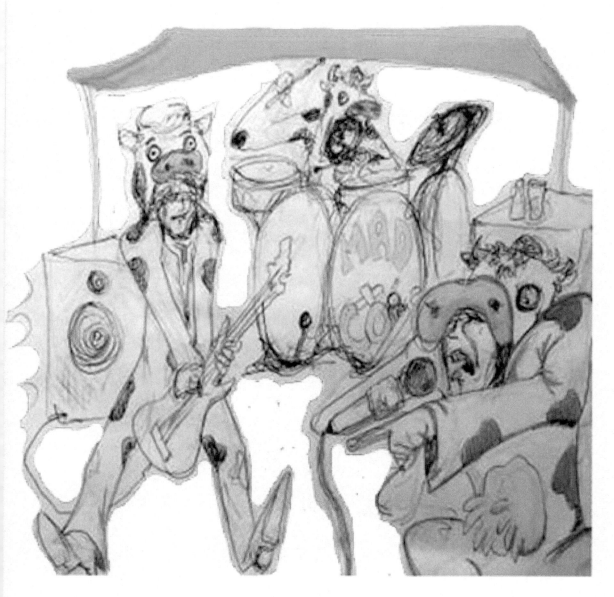

The last thing most remember of Hilly's party was of people jumping into the lake looking for a person who'd fallen in. 'Crickey . . .all we need is a dead hippy and that'll be game over for the fun times we've been having for all these years . . .'thought Lord Crust, then someone grabbed his arm . . . "It was you . . ." 'What on Earth is this nutter on about' thought a fractious Roger when he suddenly realised he was soaked right through and remembered wanting to go to bed.

Having forgotten there was a lake, Roger had only seen the path going up the hill and set off purposefully in the quickest and most direct line home.

'Strawbale Ru' – remember him . . . .? well, when working in 'Tapeley Time' things didn't just happen overnight . . .was panicking because he had a gaggle of students coming up to help put the roof on the straw bale house in 10 days' time and was far from ready . . . 'I wish I had a carpenter' thought Ru, then 10 seconds later – literally– a ginger bearded man turned up who exclaimed he "had no idea why he had come up". Rupert then asked him what line of work he was into to which 'Tony' said "I'm a carpenter". Working 12 hours a day with Rupert for 7 days and they were fully prepared for the 'students' when they finished off the strawbale house and its wonderful lean-to/veranda – all made from wood from the forest. It truly was (and still is) the 'little house on the prairie'. Tony ended up being Crustington's maintenance man and has remained so ever since. ('If only I could be more trusting' thought Roger 'and I know all will be fine so stop worrying . . .the Angels are with us every step of the way.')

It transpired that Tony had spent the previous 10 years of his life living in Saskatchewan on his own 20 miles walk from the nearest shops where temperatures regularly dropped as low as – 20℃. On returning to the UK Tony got a map of the country, shut his eyes and plonked his finger on . . . Tapeley Park, Bideford.

Tony was offered the only available (at the time) accommodation comprising a 3-foot-wide kitchen, a slate slab with no cushion, a small gas cooker to make a cup of tea – with a tiny, but cosy, mattress up a rickety old ladder (well . . . after Saskatchewan it must've felt like the Hilton to Tony).

The 'Pixie' house had been designed by a local shepherd boy just after the First World War. With no toilet, electricity and the minimalist amount of heat from a leaky wood burner, it was one way to sort out the 'wheat' from the 'chaff'. It was not as if Roger set out to make this a 'testing ground' deliberately but anyone who could put up with that degree of discomfort for 6 months or so ended up (deservedly) with their own 'space' – either in the house itself, or in an outbuilding. Many still reside in their new spaces some 10 years or so later.

Needless to say, it didn't take long for the charismatic 'Rockabilly' to woo a gorgeous local wench . . .

The day of Tony and Matilda's wedding was a stunner. With its vibrant music scene Appledore was heaven-sent for Tony who quickly became 'part of the furniture'. As such, all the local musicians and their WAGs (wives and girlfriends) came up. The dress code for the day was 'nature' which meant all the men dyed their beards different shades of green wearing costumes made out of leaves (real leaves); and the women an assortment of different coloured fairies.

The highlight for Roger was when Tony asked him if he could bring down one or two 'Highlands' to 'chivvy' things up a little . . . Roger was thrilled and waited for the last of the guests to get over the old bridge leading to the great oak.

He then got out his 2 pets 'Arthur and Nash'. A local lad called Woody had been running the elderly/overly clad down to the tree with his horse and cart creating mini hysteria in Roger's cattle the other side of the fence, so no sooner than the 2 'pets' were released than they made a beeline for the horse.

Luckily the horse had just offloaded a charming couple when Roger's boys came haring round the corner. Roger, bearing a 5 iron (golf club), and his compatriot Nikks (armed with a driver) managed to deflect the 2 Highlands to the other side of the tree from the horse.

Roger's 'boys' were by no means finished and entertained their (by now) high levels of testosterone by chucking a pile of wood (just outside the tree) into the air with their magnificent horns whilst snorting threatening moos and pulling their hooves across the ground 'suggestively' thereby stealing a fair bit of the bride and groom's thunder.

On the walk back up to the house Roger got successive rollockings from 2 elderly ladies concerning his 'immature and irresponsible' (words with which he was by now all too familiar) behaviour. Roger kindly didn't interrupt, then once they'd 'finished' gently said that the bride and groom "did ask us to bring the cattle to the wedding . . ."

With 'The Barn' packed and musicians rammed onto the stage for 12 hours solidly it was the best wedding Roger reckoned he'd been to-

-or WAS IT . . .

The aforementioned Sally Anne and Jeremy's wedding ended up being as far out as you can get.

Glastonbury Tor - the best known (along with maybe Stonehenge) beacon of light in this country- was the site selected by these 2 fully enlightened beings. A mainly Crustington crew was invited up to the Tor for their special day. Dressed up to the nines the bride then announced on the top of the Tor that the vows/declarations of love and suchlike would all be made. . . 'in silence.'

Looking deeply into one another's eyes there then proceeded a long – very long– period of 'silent vowing' during which the friends and family found it harder and harder to keep back the giggles.

The lasting memory we will all have of dear Jeremy was when (Foot and Mouth) Nikko organised a canoeing trip from inland Torrington out into the Bideford Estuary. Someone had dumped a whole load of beaten up old canoes in Crustington's back car park which were loaded into the back of Nikko's battle bus. The 'crew' found a good space to set off from but the volume of water of the turbulent river made it hard to say the least.

Sally Anne had climbed into a canoe with Jeremy who positioned himself at the rear of the canoe on a cushion holding an umbrella to keep the sun off his tender lily-white skin. Here Sally Anne, who was doing ALL the work – steering their way through the turbulence whilst feeding her beloved cucumber sandwiches and tea from a flask at the same time before getting back to the rough and tumble of the eddies- 'miraculously' negotiated their way to the safety of the Estuary.

It must be said at this juncture, that 'legends' come in many shapes, sizes and 'forms'. A 17-year-old 'boy' (he thought otherwise . . .) turned up at the Manor wanting a job in the gardens. Roger introduced this sure-footed young lad to the gardeners. The lad's face was totally engulfed in a mop of wiry ginger hair which, combined with a set of phenomenally thick spectacles, made it impossible not to stare at and disguised his real appearance perfectly. Roger relayed to the gardeners what Ben had told him . . . that he'd been working for a local attraction. Ben then said "he'd just left because his boss had been a xxxx".

This took the mini gathering aback, especially when he, turning the air even bluer, expanded upon what he'd just said (which, of course, was good enough for Roger to give him a job AND a bed in the house).

Ben was the most opinionated 17-year-old Roger had ever met (and that's saying something) he was also never wrong (an all too familiar story for many parents of teenage boys of course). The highlight of Ben's time at the Manor was his 18th birthday party. This was held at the Westleigh Inn – the pub nearest to Crustington a mere 10-minute walk across the fields, and as such, the pub of choice for all of those at the Manor.

Duncan (the new Landlord) was NOT local. He didn't speak like a local, look like a local or behave like a local.

His pinched features and shifty glances at the door, even when a car drove past, meant none of the Westleigh residents went into the pub for at least 6 months. It truly was a real life 'Royston Vasey scenario' – for those who remember the TV program. The more multicultural Crustington residents, and mostly not local themselves, were nigh on the only visitors – and certainly the only regulars– at this time. Months later, it transpired, the local's intuition proved to not be entirely unfounded.

Duncan had been involved in helping set up the rave culture in the UK and fled the London area when he heard the East End gangsters were after him because he owed money. As such, when a local did go into his pub a look of fear followed quickly by a look of huge relief, was the norm thus naturally fuelling the suspicions of the locals even more. For the crew at Crustington back then it was the best – nay 'only'– place on the map, plus you could totter home after all the fun and games . . .

As such, Ben chose to have his 18th at the Westleigh Inn Pub with the full complement of Crustington residents. Whether it was the excitement of his birthday or a rampant attempt to seduce Roger's 42 year old girlfriend (a pursuit he maintained doggedly – just dropping short of outright 'burglary') he, no doubt to impress 'Dawn', necked a terrifying looking jet black substance

causing every vein in his eyes to burst as 'Ring of Fire' blared out on the pub gramophone.

2 days later it was the popular landlord's 40th birthday. With a pub rammed with locals, musicians and Morris dancers 'Boy Wonder' (AKA Leon and resident of The Crust) as the blonde 'waitress' was known, knocked up a 'concoction' enough to bring a rhinoceros down.

20 minutes after the 'obliging' landlord passed out, a local doctor pumped his heart back into action and he was off to A and E with his distraught sobbing Mum at his side.

The lovely 18year old softly spoken 'enri' (who'd lived and 'worked' at the Manor for 2 years) was not a boat rocker, but a really civilised wholesome person who simply wanted a quiet life. However, one fine spring day, Roger did manage to entice 'enri' out of his comfort zone . . .

A Norwegian camera crew had rung up Daphne to say that they were in the West Country making a documentary about all things quintessentially 'English' and wondered if 'Crustington' may be able to lay something on for them to film. Suggestions ranged from filming couples having a cream tea to filming the volunteers in the gardens. When Roger heard this request he quickly came up with, what he considered, was a much better idea and told the Norwegians he'd explain once they arrived at Crustington to which they, if a little confused, agreed.

No sooner had Lord Crust put the phone down than off he went in search of 'enri'. The modest 18-year-old was acclaimed as one of the top 'skater' kids in North Devon and a regular visitor to Bideford's 'legendary' (well . . .to those in the know) half pipe.

Roger found the obliging 'enri 'working' in the vegetable garden (he was part of a rare breed at Crustington at that time as folk may have gathered by now) and asked if he might come to the house where he had a 'proposal.' Roger took 'enri' into the kitchen where he met the film crew and suggested to both parties his idea . . . 'The Bull Terrier Challenge . . .'

Most people know that Bull Terriers are the most obsessive of all dogs on the planet. Bryan (Roger's then 4-year-old EBT)'s 'Biggest' obsession (he had a few . . .) was skateboards. Bryan just had to see a skateboard and he'd go apoplectic. Roger and his South African buddy, Doug, would take it in 'turns' to do the challenge. One would hold Bryan by the collar whilst the other faced the skateboard down towards Daphne's shop – the idea being to get in a sharp left hand 'bottom turn' on the right-angled bend at the bottom of the hill. They'd give each other a 20-yard start before releasing the frantic barking beast – so as such it was a genuine achievement to get in the sharp bottom turn and remain unscathed.

52

Bryan was very good because he'd always go for the skateboard and wheels — not the foolish idiot on the board at the time.

One fine morning an exceedingly posh gentleman, wearing a tweed jacket with a red and white spotted handkerchief neatly peeking out of the upper left small pocket of aforesaid jacket, came out of the car park onto the drive at the same time as Roger was lining up for the tricky bottom near right angle turn. Bryan took Roger out more spectacularly than usual in that as Roger got knocked for six, the skateboard spun up vertically and Roger took the full blast in his nether regions.

The 'gentleman', who we assumed later was probably the Chairman of the William Morris Society — though that's not exactly fair to William Morris— gave the groaning Lord of the Manor a look of disdain and contempt the likes of which Donald Trump would have been proud of.

When Roger and Doug came up with the idea of dressing 'enri' in Lord Crust's cricket whites armed with cricket gloves and cricket bat and sending him down the longer (and steeper) main drive, 'enri' didn't take to the idea with any enthusiasm whatsoever. Quite the opposite in fact, much to the huge disappointment of the 2 more elderly men.

However, after a few kind words, bribes (and the obvious thrill about appearing on Norwegian TV) and the dashing, daring 'enri' agreed, albeit still very reluctantly, to do it.

Excitement levels were at fever pitch as the 2 organisers were positioning the 2 Norwegian cameramen at the optimal position to get the best shots of this extreme thrill seeking English pastime. Neither Doug or Roger noticed the look of utter confusion on the 2 Norwegian's faces - they were too busy getting the out and out 'star' of the show padded (and 'boxed' - yes, no stone was left unturned) up.

The historic moment was upon all with Bryan's bark sounding louder and more hysterical than ever as he no doubt sensed the specialness of this event. As such the organisers/perpetrators gave 'enri' a good head start, and, they felt, a fighting chance of not only out manoeuvring the EBT but outrunning/skating him.

'Enri' was travelling as fast as the wheels could possibly function without flying off when Bryan made the UIC (ultimate impact connection). Photographic evidence shows poor 'enri' flying in the air before ending up on his back on the tarmac. Thankfully the injuries and grazes weren't too bad – nothing a bit of terps couldn't put right – this also to reduce the risk of infection as well. We know what folk will be thinking . . . 'Roger and Doug's thoughtfulness knows no bounds'.

The problem was that in the melee and excitement the Englishman and South African hadn't thought how the Norwegians might be feeling whilst viewing this 'quintessentially English' past time and on looking round noticed their jaws were 'quite literally' on the floor (or, in this case, tarmac). Before the pulsatingly excited duo had a chance to tell them the next excellent idea for their TV program, the Norwegians had packed up and were off down the drive.

When Bryan passed on, Roger waited for a good while before seeking out another dog. Roger felt he was 'doing the breed' a favour by giving a 'rescue' dog a good home. 'Bruce' was a large, handsome brown and white EBT aged 7 from South Devon, and needed a home. Within hours of arriving Bruce had divided the community right down the middle.

EBT - English Bull Terrier

Bruce was a lump but like all Bull Terriers he was never going to lie anywhere other than on someone's lap. To Roger, he was the answer to a dream but the writing on the wall suggested otherwise when the bull terrier jumped up and bit a baby. Thankfully, it just caused some minor bruising, but tears flowed like the River Jordan when the rather irate lady came up from South Devon to take Bruce away.

Next stop 'Scooby' . . .If Bruce was a demented crocodile then Scooby was a sabre-toothed tiger. Scooby was all white and as such another Bryan in Roger's overly soppy eyes. Roger drove across the country to West Sussex to meet, greet and ultimately take Scooby back to Devon.

The good news was 'that this time the baby didn't get it . . .' but pretty much everyone else did. Jenny, Crustington's Permaculture Queen in residence, was at her wits end and on the verge of leaving – such was her understandable fear for her precious pooches 'Bruno and Bella', and it didn't take long for her (and the overzealous Roger) to find out she had a genuine point.

It was new(ish) arrival Debbie's 30th. Scooby was locked away behind 2 separate doors. Someone, however, had taken pity on the howling Bull Terrier and no doubt 'in kindness' let the poor dog out. Natasha was a lovely lady and brilliant masseur who lived locally at the aptly named 'Hartland' some 10 or so miles away.

Natasha had her beautiful, gentle Irish wolf hound cross bitch with her lolling around the fire pit.

It was then we witnessed the damaged side of Scooby as he (having broken through 2 firmly shut doors in the house) literally tore chunks out of the poor dog. Natasha did what any loving mother would do and put her hand down to protect her dog only to see her hand erupt with blood. Roger, of course, duly coughed up the £1,500 in lieu of medical costs and lost earnings, and thankfully Natasha made a full recovery and was grateful to Roger for compensating her fully.

Roger had (at last, some might say) learnt his lesson and in 2015, obtained a gorgeous brown and white EBT puppy from Yeovil called Wayne (after his football captain). Wayne was as good as gold whilst maintaining his traditional 'terrier' like qualities of razzing up Highland cattle at every opportunity and going ballistic at skateboards.

It had, by now, been a good 10 years since Roger had let in the angry German 'Gerhard' into the bosom of the Crust, and felt it high time to give the 'ones we love to hate' another crack . . .

First there was Dieter - a vegan and part time 'juggler' . . .One fine spring day Doug invited the motley crew down to the 'hut' for a barbeque. Dieter repeatedly informed everybody of his nutritional demands to ensure there was no cross-contamination, and Doug (an extreme meat eater verging on the Jurassic) kindly prepared a vegan option for Doug and the other vegetarians. Doug, being the bullish, but caring, South African he so clearly was, (without thinking) seeing the veggie pot needed a stir, thoughtfully (in the South African sense), removed the large wooden spoon from the venison, wild rabbit and squirrel mix (all in plentiful supply in the woods) and gave Dieter's veggie concoction a damn good stir.

There was no pulling the wool over the eyes of the sensitive German – "von Dunkov has put zi spoon from zi meat pot into my pot?"– who with his poor, but lovely, son then packed his bags and set off down the drive.

The next German to grace the palatial grounds was Johan. Johan was a 'worker' from the 'Wavey Davey' stable but with twice the anger. Because of this, the 2 (understandably)grumpy old gardeners on the terraces banished Johan to the then dumping ground in 'Permaculture' to work with Jenny. Jenny was one of the most patient, kind people you could ever have the privilege to meet but even she, after one shift, sent him back to where he'd just come from where he was (inevitably)then told to go back to Permaculture, and from there back to Germany.

A few years later Johan, Beatrice and their 3 adorable very young daughters came to a Didgeridoo Festival (a major source of recruitment for activists and 'inmates'- for a good 15 years as you may have gathered). Amongst all the rough and ready yet charming tepees, traveller's trucks, tents and the rest, there stood the most adorable multi-coloured truck Roger had ever seen. Intrigued, Roger approached said truck and found the inhabitants to be as delectably delicious as the paintwork on the truck.

When the Didge field emptied on the Bank Holiday Monday evening, the Germans, to the delight of Roger, asked if they could stay on for a bit. Roger allowed them to keep their pitch in the field adding to the picturesque view for him and the visitors to the park. Even the Highland cattle roaming around freely amongst the adults and children seemed uncharacteristically calm and 'tangibly' respectful of their new neighbours where Roger also noticed a protective energy exuding from the cattle. In the 6 months they were there, they created all sorts of sculptures out of the flotsam and jetsam in the woods. This included stiles at the entrance of the permaculture garden, a well-thought-out woodland walk and a seat fit for a king, made from the stump of a massive ash, by Roger's backdoor.

Doug had first come to Crustington Manor for a stag weekend for
Christian - a member of an all family Festival band called the
'Mad Cows'. The band was fronted by Hamish - the maddest 'cow' of
the lot, who were regulars at The Big Green Gathering, Glastonbury,
the Secret Garden Party etc. where they were always dressed as
cows.

Being that there was already a party in the Barn, the gathering for the cows took place at the not quite finished straw bale house. At 2am Lord Crust felt it time to liven up the stags who had by then sunk into singing a series of non-decipherable drunken melodies so Roger assertively announced "We need to move the Highland cattle" "what, now?" replied a less intoxicated cow, "yes, they've eaten all their grass and will be hungry and cross in the morning."

The motley crew of giggling 'cows' stumbled to their feet, much to the amazement of Roger, but when they saw through the moonlight what they were being asked to get into the field with, they went very quiet indeed. Lord Crust, by then himself beginning to wonder if this was really a good idea, began issuing firm orders centred around the importance of them all holding a straight line, "wave your arms in the air and shout if they come towards you and most important of all, don't run if they charge you – it'll only get them more excited and you need to let them know who's boss or you could get hurt . . ." (A vet once told Roger that Highland cows kill more farmers than all the other breeds put together, but LC wisely refrained from releasing this piece of information).

Roger then selected a couple of the more sober fitter looking 'cows' to go in front of the cattle with him through a gate past a stream and the children's play area, round the permaculture garden and right onto the drive and from there into the Monument Park. The cattle had done this route many times before and with a full moon in the sky and all the help a herdsman (as LC referred to himself when asked his 'occupation') could possibly have, surely things couldn't have been simpler . . .?

Whether it was the effects of the full moon or the vibes of the now silent and petrified stags - most of whom were edging their way back towards the fence in a rather cowardly fashion (or so the rather brazen LC thought), the Highlands became friskier than usual.

Suddenly, led by Mel, the cattle charged. The 2 'stags' with LC leapt over a fence and Roger ran for all his worth to keep ahead of them but ended up in the stream in the dark.

The gate leading onto the drive was open. The cattle 'knew' their way to the monument field, having done the route many times- only this time instead of turning right up the drive they turned left and stampeded towards the main road.

The hapless Roger watched pathetically as the last of his cattle tore around the corner some 200 metres away towards the busy main road chased solely by Saffey - a 14-year-old girl who (Roger thought) had about as much chance of halting the stampede as King Canute halting the incoming tide.

In Roger's experience, when they hit the main road, they tended to split with some going right towards the small village of Instow and the others going left towards Bideford. LC had had many brushes with the law during Foot and Mouth and even been to prison for his beliefs, but, this time, he knew he'd behaved with inexcusable immaturity and could be in real trouble, especially if somebody got hurt. A good 5 or so minutes later the 'brave' stags, having crept out from their hideouts, sheepishly appeared at Roger's side. ('Now the so called "Mad Cows" really know what it means to be a 'Mad Cow'' thought LC.)

With real trouble ahead, as if by 'magic', the cattle suddenly came bombing round the corner back up the drive closely followed by Saffey.

The 14-year-old girl told us she had managed to overtake the cattle in the woods, then leap onto the drive by the bottom gate at the same time the cattle arrived, put out her hands and yelled 'STOOOOPPPP.'

The image of a scene from a Tom and Jerry cartoon comes to mind with the cattle digging their front hooves into the tarmac. The cows (human ones) themselves, far from hanging their heads in shame at their outright cowardice, took off all their clothes and performed a dance in the style of African warriors who'd managed to bring down a buffalo.

Roger set sail for a holiday early the next day - his first for 5 years, to the Alps. The hippies allowed, on Roger's return, one night of peace and relaxation before breaking the news that no sooner than Roger had driven down the drive than the cattle broke out. Having passed the 'Great Oak' they plundered through a barbed wire fence over a fast-flowing stream onto Morris Dart's land. Being that there was no grass to graze they made their way towards the village of Westleigh.

Having 'negotiated' a five-foot bank and a barbed wire fence, they set about filling their bellies with an array of succulent vegetables courtesy of the locals' allotments.

Roger was a keen advocate of good Karma (wherever possible) and not only promised the locals they would be fairly compensated but also led a posse up to the damaged allotments and set about digging up the hoof prints and putting topsoil followed by vegetable seeds across the damaged area. But . . . the problem hadn't just gone away . . . Whilst on their 'travels' the cattle had clearly 'clocked' the lush green grass growing in abundance, along with the frail/rusty wrought iron gate, leading into the 'Westleigh graveyard'. Roger feared the worst when he walked the fields by the drive and the cattle were nowhere to be seen.

If the hoof prints were considered deep after their first trip to the allotments, the prints left after the second trip were twice as deep – this due to the phenomenal fertility of the untouched (dare one say it) 'virginal' rich soil. The only gravestone to come out unscathed was (ironically) where Roger's Grandfather and Grandmother were buried (where, such was the thickness of the granite, not even a modern day 'grave robber', or nuclear bomb for that matter, would be capable of penetrating the surrounding stone).

It took 3 large trailer loads of good topsoil to fill up the three-foot-deep hoof prints – even the plastic flowers laid for the more recently deceased, didn't escape the appetite of the, by then, rampant cattle who were gorging on everything bar the tombstones themselves. The whole tidy up took 8+ people all of 2 weeks to restore the graveyard for which Roger and 'friends' got a write up of thanks in the WESTLEIGH PARISH NEWSLETTER. 'Karma restored' and off went Roger to see his beloved Mum and have a well-earned rest.

THE END... (for now)

APPENDIX

Roger had always loved farm animals - cattle in particular from as far back as he could remember. (He also had a 'penchant' for standing on a tiny ledge outside his bedroom window - always on a full moon- until one day he got back from school only to find his windows barred up to the hilt). A 'seed 'was sown and Roger worked on farms from the age of 13 onwards - where he took on many jobs, and even killed turkeys by hand. Well. . . you've gotta start somewhere.

As mentioned, Roger loved to have a 'pet' in tow whether it be a lamb called 'no-name', Highland cattle like Arthur, Harold or Martha (details of Martha's miraculous recovery on website . . .) BUT . . . the cherry on the cake had to be . . . 'Christmas'.

When Roger opened the curtains on Christmas day the first thing he saw was a goose gently walking across the front lawn. Intrigued, Roger went outside to meet his new guest. Instead of walking away Christmas, head down with bright orange eyes (matching her beautiful bright orange webbed feet) went for Roger and drew blood through his jeans. This, fortunately for Roger, was the only time he was bitten by her (when a goose bites you, to maximise the pain inflicted, they bite and twist at the same time). As such, Roger was a little disappointed that Christmas hadn't turned up a day or so earlier as most of the crew would have preferred a succulent, moist slice of goose breast (vegetarians aside) to a dry, manky old bit of turkey breast.

Christmas loathed all things female – whether that be a cow, bitch, ewe – you name it. Parents visiting the park were firmly instructed to walk the other way if Christmas went onto the lawn where people were having picnics or simply playing with their children.

It got to the stage when, under extreme pressure from sensible people up at Tapeley – namely Daphne, Christmas had to be popped into a pen in the day and only let out when the last members of the public had left.

Roger was seriously considering some sort of 'exit' plan re. The goose, as she wasn't contributing much to the party. Whenever she was let out, once the public had left, she'd attack all the female gardeners – some of whom were saying they were going to leave – when the first of two miracles occurred . . .

With Christmas safely locked up in her pen, Roger went looking for help to get the cattle moved. The cattle in the Monument field were nigh on horizontally passive and, with a bucket-full of scrumptious cattle-nuts and not much grass around, Roger reckoned they would easily follow him to the fresh grass by the drive as they'd done many times before.

    As Roger approached the drive, something spooked the Highlands and they began stampeding in all directions around Roger's largest field . . . Roger, arms flailing, whooping frantically heard the 'Rah Rah' as Christmas flew at a 45° angle rising above the massive Monterey pines landing hard in the field on her huge chest bouncing like something in the 'Dambusters' movie. She then, standing tall, flapped her wings giving a series of 'Rah Rah's' and single-handedly herded the troublesome cattle out of the field, down the drive and into the field of Roger's choice.

A week or so later, Roger was asked by the local school if he would do a talk for a 100 or so youngsters with learning difficulties. As Roger neared the barn, the noise levels escalated to something resembling a Globalise Resistance planning convention. Roger realised he had to pull the proverbial 'rabbit out of the hat' if he were to win his audience over and said he would be back in ten minutes.

Roger sprinted down to the woods and got the goose out of her pen. When Roger got her into the small Bar area of the barn, Christmas let out her loudest ever 'Rah Rah' and all went deadly quiet in a matter of seconds. Roger climbed the few steps into the barn with the goose following 'pat pat pat' behind him.

Following a second 'Rah Rah', Christmas leapt on top of Roger's lap where Roger announced a last-minute change to the planned schedule because . . . "today will be hosted by our special guest . . . CHRISTMAS."

Word got around the local community like wildfire and 'school outings' booked left right and centre (keeping it quiet from 'ealth n' safety, obviously. . .) If Roger went banging on too long Christmas would stand up on his lap, flap her wings and bang out a couple of 'Rah Rah's' getting the attention back to the Star of the show.

Christmas became the hottest property on the circuit and entertained children and parents alike until she passed away in old age.

P.S. First names ONLY have been used to 'reduce' the risk of 'suing'.

P.P.S. For 'more of the same' (in some ways) see: The Final Curtain Call.

For something completely different, try Roger's first book: No Blade of Grass . . .' (is blown without 'Divine Intention').

P.P.P.S. If you can't be 'good' be careful, and if you can't be careful, remember the date (RIP Gordon Steer).

Wayne

Brian

A FOREWORD

This is a 'raw' account

Of 'Agri Activism'

and our fight to produce healthy, wholesome food fir our families.

The battle at times has been severe

but at least we are seeing the Light at the end of the tunnel.

Please forgive the rawness of our delivery .

it cuts into our soul.

Thank you

When my semi-professional football career was suddenly terminated in Feb 2001 by a clumsy 16 stone centre-half at Bath (double tib . . .), I wondered what on earth that was for . . ? (I'd believed that there's a 'reason' for everything for a while and written a book about it), then 10 days later whilst (bored) watching lunch time TV, the presenter announced "Foot and Mouth was spreading up from Holsworthy and Hatherleigh towards North Devon . . ." It was my 'Eureka moment.' 'That's why my leg was broken . . . I need to put all my energy into saving my and other's animals . . .'

I was the first farmer to padlock and chain my gates

for the next 6 months I was literally at war with MAFF. Farmers would ring me at any time of day or night and I'd mobilise people – often at 3am who we'd picked up en route in an ex-army lorry emblazoned with CULL MAFF to the delight of the poor local farmer whose animals were due for slaughter – often at dawn before the solicitors/legal team were up.

We had no idea how radicle we'd become – locking arms against the police, army, Trading Standards, MAFF; felling trees across access routes and placing 'human shields' in hedgerows to stop slaughtermen shooting from the hip causing stampedes as they jumped into neighbouring fields thereby increasing the cull. To cap it all I received a leaked document from a MAFF official which stated that the FMD vaccine was 99% efficient and there was enough for all the animals in the UK. The reason for the slaughter was for the 'export market' of animals packed into crates like sardines.

This made me angry and before I knew it I was off to G8 summits (boy Genoa was scary in 2001), heckling Prime Ministers – starting with Tony Blair . . . ., stopping a Tesco being built in our local town, pulling GM wheat crops in Roathamstead Research Centre and pulling my trousers down on breakfast TV (much to the horror of Adrian Charles and Natasha Kaplinski – especially). (The Glyndebourne costume department have been extremely helpful turning me into the vegetable of my choice). I've run out of a little steam recently but am helping to try to get Roundup 'a probable carcinogen' A/C the WTO and other pesticides like 'neo-nics' off shop shelves.

I'm giving you this in the hope you might be able to help me in some way – whether it be guidance, ideas, contact details of people who feel the same or whatever. These are precarious times, and when I'm on my deathbed I don't want my children to say to me . . . ."Dad, when you knew so much about what's going on why didn't you do more to help?"

JNTRY NEWS ● WESTERN MORNING NEWS ● FRIDAY NOVEMBER 11 2005

Author bases book on experiences of his campaign to highlight threat of globalisation

Crusader's first novel comes with a message

MARK CLOUGH

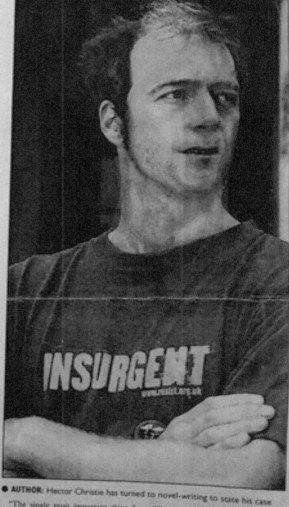

● **AUTHOR:** Hector Christie has turned to novel-writing to state his case

A CAMPAIGNING Westcountry landowner whose battles with authority have seen him brought before the courts and ejected from the Labour Party conference, has written a novel to help him get his message across.

Hector Christie wrote "The Final Curtain Call" to highlight his fears about the growing threat of globalisation. Although written as a novel, the book draws heavily on his experiences in fighting the causes he believes in so passionately.

Mr Christie, whose stately home at Tapeley Park in North Devon offers commanding views across the Taw-Torridge estuary, hit the headlines during the dark days of foot and mouth in 2001 with his bitter condemnation of the actions of the Ministry of Agriculture, Fisheries and Food (MAFF), which later became the Department for Environment, Food and Rural Affairs (Defra).

He staged a traffic blockade in Bideford to highlight his opposition to the ministry's culling plans and vowed to barricade his land against ministry officials should they come to cull his own animals.

He also joined farmers at their gates as they sought to protect their livestock from the massive culling programme.

More recently, Mr Christie, whose family run the internationally-famous Glyndebourne Opera Festival, was ejected from the 2004 Labour Party conference in Brighton for heckling Tony Blair over the war in Iraq.

Earlier this year he interrupted a speech being given by Chancellor Gordon Brown in Scotland. Protesting about the mounting debt of third world countries, kilt-wearing Mr Christie raised his garment to reveal a Tony Blair "codpiece".

Now, Mr Christie has turned to novel-writing to get his message out.

The Final Curtain Call is set in 2020 and tells the story of Devon farmer Harold Smith through the eyes of his daughter, Annie, and his own diaries. Although it features the sombre topics of cattle culls and an increasingly authoritarian state, Mr Christie said he had tried to inject humour and hope into the book.

"It is a heavy topic and something I have been campaigning about rather

> **'I hope this will give people more hope and help them really believe'**

frantically, and even in desperation, these past few years," he said.

"However, I've tried to make it a fun read and a book to give hope to those who read it."

Alongside the weighty topics of genetically modified crops and the Iraq war, Mr Christie said he had also tried to get over a spiritual element to his campaigning.

"I hope this will give people more hope and help them really believe and know that everything we all do, no matter how big or small, will make an enormous difference," he said.

"I believe if we don't do something, there isn't going to be much of a world for our children and grandchildren.

"The single most important thing I learnt during our foot and mouth protests was how unbelievably powerful we all are."

The book has won praise from leading environmentalists since being published.

Former Environment Secretary Michael Meacher, who campaigned with Mr Christie against GM crops, said: "Hector is determined, caring and fun, as well as mocking of authority.

"He may have been born with a silver spoon in his mouth, but my God he cares about the world and doing his best to make it a better place."

Profits from the book will go to the Save Our World charity that Mr Christie set up to help end global poverty.

● Mr Christie will be signing copies of his book at Walter Henry's Bookshop in High Street, Bideford, tomorrow, from 11am to 2pm.

GM crops in England as soon as next year

Outrage as ministers back first commercial planting

By Sean Poulter
Consumer Affairs Editor

ANTI-GM campaigners reacted with fury last night after the Government backed an EU vote that could lead to weed-killer-resistant maize being sowed in England next year.

Other European countries can ban the so-called Frankenstein food after EU ministers said members could opt out of GM planting.

Critics said England's first commercial GM crops would spell disaster for wildlife and contaminate conventional and organic crops, with 'catastrophic' consequences for farmers.

The Government position is also at odds with those of the Scottish Parliament and the Welsh Assembly, which have opted for a ban.

The EU vote allowing the planting of two types of maize resistant to the weedkiller Roundup was passed by agriculture ministers in Luxembourg, although the European Parliament

'Colluding with lobbyists'

must approve it. Dr Helen Wallace, of the campaign group GeneWatch UK, said: 'The Government has colluded with commercial lobbyists to fast track Roundup Ready GM maize into England, despite the expected harm to British wildlife such as birds and butterflies caused by blanket spraying of these crops.

'If some farmers in England press ahead with GM cultivation, conventional and organic farmers across the country will face the unnecessary risk of loss of markets due to contamination with GM.'

The Government's pro-GM stance also flies in the face of public opinion, with most consumers saying they are concerned about the impact of the crops on the countryside, wildlife and their health.

The approval of commercial GM planting has been stalled for ten years because the EU needed all member states to vote for it.

Environment Secretary Owen Paterson – the Government's cheerleader for genetically-modified crops – has been pressing for regulations that allow individual member states to plant them once they have been declared safe by Brussels.

He said the EU decision will fast-track them into farms and supermarkets, adding: 'This is a real step forward in unblocking the dysfunctional EU process for approving GM crops, which is letting down farmers and stopping scientific development.

'Farmers will have more power in deciding whether to grow GM crops that have passed a robust, independent safety assessment.'

But Peter Melchett, of organic industry body the Soil Association, said: 'In future, a committed, pro-GM Secretary of State like Owen Paterson could take the decision to make England a "GM country", and once that is taken it will be difficult for a future Government to adopt a different position. This will lead to farmers losing export markets to the rest of Europe and most of the rest of the world, which would be catastrophic.'

The EU vote is a victory for multi-national biotech firms, which have spent millions lobbying British ministers and officials to speed up the approval of GM crops. The Government claims there is no risk to humans or the environment.

But European and US research suggests there are health concerns and a threat to wildlife, and warns of the damage from 'superweeds' that develop a natural resistance to the pesticides used on GM crops.

Liz O'Neill, director of GM Freeze, said: 'Even if a country or region does establish a ban, they will find it very difficult to protect their fields and food from contamination if neighbours start growing GM.'

However, the Government said safeguards would be put in place to protect conventional crops from GM contamination.

How the Frankenfood giants got their way

[column partially illegible]

cont:.

in the trade press. The policy states that, while evidence and advice from scientific and government bodies and indeed the wider food industry is generally taken into account that the decision to avoid GM products has been enforced as a matter of customer choice, based on our understanding of the wide public's view on the issue.

We hope this answer is of help to you.

Yours sincerely,
Robert Twigger
Secretary of the Commission.

Charter of the Faucheurs Volontaires
Say NO to GMO's
Not in our Fields, Not on our Plates
The Faucheurs Volontaires are committed to neutralising these pesticide plants. They commit open, public acts of civic disobedience, non-violently, respecting the integrity of all citizens. They target only those commodities which threaten the public good.
The Faucheurs Volontaires organise their own actions, for which they publically take responsibility.

- having to buy their seed EVERY year - (farmers some of the poorest in the world caught saving their seed are prosecuted).
- "'Golden Rice' with extra vitamin A will feed the third world and help ward off blindness . . ." Nice idea but it's impossible physically to eat enough of the stuff to make any difference (planting and eating more spinach plus selecting the natural weeds growing amongst the crops perm culture style - as the Indians had always done until Roundup came along and zapped the lot, would soon . sort that one).
- In the 50's smoking was practically encouraged as 'good for you'. In the 60's DDT was deemed safe and sprayed liberally. Likewise now Monsanto still advocate the safety of Roundup (and the GM crops) and have just developed a crop that is resistant to 2-4D - Agent Orange . . .

- April 22nd 2014 . . . . 'RUSSIAN PRIME MINISTER DMITRY MEDVEDEV ANNOUNCED THAT RUSSIA WILL NOT IMPORT ANY MORE GMO FOOD PRODUCTS OR SEED' . . . 'Prominent Russian scientists declare that a moratorium should be imposed on GMO's for at least 10 years.' This to ascertain safety to it's people and the environment citing the recent alarming results of Dr. Seralini's testing on rats.

Closer to home . . . .on June 22nd 2013 an article by the Deputy Political Editor of the Telegraph states "GM KEPT OFF THE MENU AT WESTMINSTER." What message does this put out other than, "It's OK to POISON all of us but not the elite in Parliament"? We felt this state of affairs needed verification so kindly Michael Meacher MP asked a question to this effect on 15.5.2014 and he received the following response:-

15th May 2014. Mr. Michael Meacher MP,
House of Commons, London. SW1A 0AA

Dear Mr. Meacher,
On 12th May you tabled a named day PQ to the House of Commons Commission for answer today, Thursday 15th May. As prorogation occurred yesterday the question has fallen, however, a response was prepared and may be of use to you.

You asked whether GM food is sold in re... the House Catering Services GM p... of GM foods. This is no on ethi... but reflects current public views...

20th May 2014
If GMOs are harmless, why are they not eating them in Westminster?
Demand to know what is in your food, how and where it was produced - and who made the profit
We are entitled to OPEN and FRANK debate on the pros and cons of GMO
WE ARE WHAT WE EAT
JUST SAY NO! TO GMO

- Indeed in every aspect of GM there's a sinister dark side slickly covered up by their entourage of extremely well paid scientists and lobbyists . . . .
- As a farmer in the 1990's I, like most others, liberally sprayed Monsanto's Roundup on pesky weeds which destroyed the little blighters roots and all . . . .
- Last year, in the same way Australian scientist Jack Heinaman from the University of Canterbury expressed concerns from tests of potential 'major health problems' in wheat Frederique Baudouin published an article in the high ranked Scientific Journal 'Toxicology' about 'safety studies' on Roundup. In the states "the health and environmental agencies and pesticide companies assess the long-term effects on mammals of GLYPHOSATE (an ingredient of 'Roundup' – the less toxic compound) ALONE. However, the complete mix contains added ingredients = ADJUVANTS. These are classified as INERT but without these the glyphosate would not be stabilised enough to help penetrate the thick (cellular) walls (i.e. without this Roundup wouldn't work) . . . .the health and environmental agencies and pesticide companies assess the long-term effects on mammals of GLYPHOSATE ALONE ."
- Much of our groundwater in the UK contains traces, to a greater or less degree, of the poison Roundup.
- Roundup is sprayed over crops ('drifting' into communities) from the AIR in some parts of South America.
- Dr Seralini's rats fed traces of Roundup showed the same high ratio of tumours as those fed GM.

- Does our Government care? Not when it receives £250million from the BBSRC (the Biotech industry), according to the (little known) Green Food Project Conclusions document on May 24th 2012 4 days after that fellow scaled the fence at Rothampstead Research Centre, where he scattered organic wheat seed and pulled a few GM wheat plants causing people to discuss the potential dangers of putting (effectively) a cow gene into a wheat plant to ward off aphids?
- We implore you to watch 'GMcropsfarmertofarmer.com' 'Genetic Roulette' and 'seeds of change' on the net to get more of the grim picture on the effects of growing GM in the US on American farmers - likewise the story of 'Percy Schmeisser'. More recent DVD's shows alarming evidence of the effects on adults AND children-with farmers and parents stating that the health of their animals and children respectively noticeably improved after just 3 days of reverting to a non GM diet.
- 'How else can we Feed the World . .? Indian writer and activist, Vandana Shiva, states that more then 250,000 Indian farmers have committed suicide as a result of crop failure AND

Farmers interviewed state that they deeply regret being coerced into growing GM crops, and now they are 'hooked' in they can't back out. They state that in huge tracts of America there are no conventional seed manufacturers left, and their margins are plummeting.

- This they say is because after 3 or so years the (BT) insecticide's and herbicide's (roundup) effectiveness at suppressing pests and weeds

respectively dramatically reduces. Farmers show the super-weeds growing in their fields which need to be pulled by hand by cheap Mexican labour. The (obvious) point being that if you apply the same herbicide or insecticide, nature mutates and resistance builds up which is why we use different malarial pills, sheep wormer and so on. GM is a one trick pony.

TOXICITY

Monsanto's Roundup was marketed as the cure-all answer to the weed problem applied just once onto bare ground. However, now it is sprayed up to 5 times a year - 4 passes of which will go directly onto the growing crop and thence straight into our food chain. US and Canadian farmers are applying powerful tank mixes of roundup, 24-D and atrazine(the latter 2 banned in Europe) but even with this potent cocktail success is sporadic. Monsanto have patented this tank mix, so if farmers get caught mixing their own they get prosecuted.

Not only is it getting much harder and more costly to keep yields to a reasonable level in the US and Canada but in poorer countries such as India where GM crops are now everywhere (Monsanto used famous 'Bollywood' actors to persuade farmers to grow GM), the human suffering resulting from higher costs and no benefits has escalated exponentially.

Vandana Shiva in a recent resurgence Magazine states that "the debt trap created by farmers being forced to buy seed every year, with crippling royalty payments, has pushed hundreds of thousands of farmers to suicide - 250,000 to date."

I believe it's not possible to say that this figure is all attributable to GM - many poor Indian farmers have tragically committed suicide each year due to crop failure, drought and so on. However, Monsanto inserting the 'terminator gene' into seed, preventing some of the poorest farmers in the world from saving seed and forcing them to go back to Monsanto each year is, to me, a crime against humanity of the highest order.

A Rothampstead scientist described (on radio 4 on 12.6.12) these terminator seeds as 'need to purchase seeds' which are sold in Africa and India' along with all the other types of seed' - no mention of the 'T'.

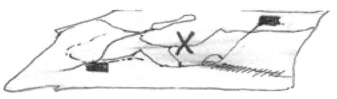

A colleague had sent me a map with a few photos to give a clue as to where the trial was located. This was absolutely no use whatsoever since the map was very small, blurred and impossible to read. It did, however, have pictures of Rothampstead Research Centre itself and a random picture of a number plate – which to me gave no useful info whatsoever and as such seemed pointless (but I believe it was this 'evidence' that attracted the police from London who grilled me that evening. I don't think they would have been bothered otherwise – I barely did any damage).

NO ENTRY

With a bit of organic wheat seed in a bag (having seen the fence I knew I wouldn't be able to take in much seed) which I hoped to scatter to make a token gesture, I set off. The fence was one hundred metres or so away from the woodland I was in. The area around it had been clear felled so as not to obstruct views of the CCTV cameras liberally scattered around the perimeter. I walked around the gates with endless warnings in red without reading anything. I didn't want to become too scared and bottle it. I walked towards the nearest CCTV camera on the corner, expecting the security guards I could see around the fence to leap into their van and take me away. To be honest, I was hoping beyond hope this is exactly what would happen. I'd have made my point and had a little story I could get out to increase public awareness as to what was going on.

As I walked around the perimeter I (rather relieved) couldn't think how on earth I could get in. I didn't have any bolt cutters, but not even they'd have worked because the fence had been designed to prevent this by having the mesh packed in so close together (plus I didn't wish to get into trouble for having such things on me).

After dithering around for a while waiting for security to come and get me, I wandered across a track in full view of 2 security guards, standing next to their vehicle, into a wood. Whist still expecting (hoping) to hear the security approaching I started looking for a piece of wood to stand on – 'maybe I was supposed to get in' I thought? I went out of the forest with a piece of wood that was no good, so ditched it and went back to get a better bit – thinking 'surely they must have seen me by now.' Eventually I found a rotten old stump, pointed at the end.

(Before attempting to get in, I chucked a fertiliser bag half full of seed over the fence without it breaking – the 'first' miracle).

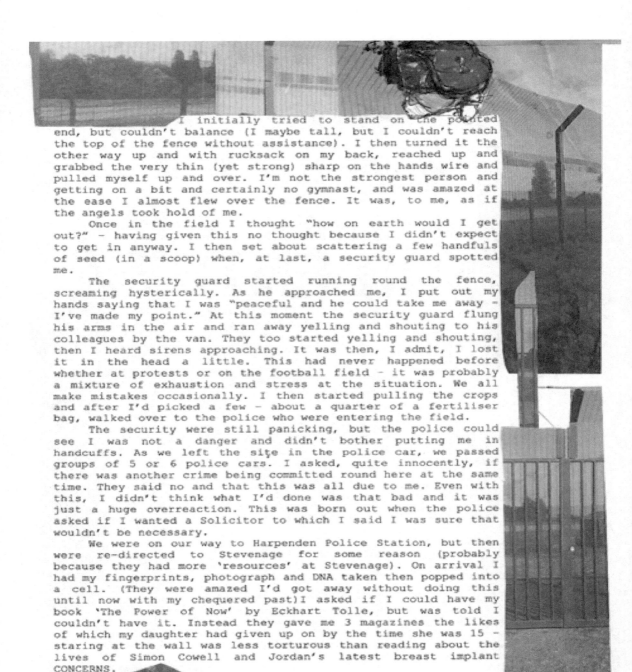

I initially tried to stand on the pointed end, but couldn't balance (I maybe tall, but I couldn't reach the top of the fence without assistance). I then turned it the other way up and with rucksack on my back, reached up and grabbed the very thin (yet strong) sharp on the hands wire and pulled myself up and over. I'm not the strongest person and getting on a bit and certainly no gymnast, and was amazed at the ease I almost flew over the fence. It was, to me, as if the angels took hold of me.

Once in the field I thought "how on earth would I get out?" - having given this no thought because I didn't expect to get in anyway. I then set about scattering a few handfuls of seed (in a scoop) when, at last, a security guard spotted me.

The security guard started running round the fence, screaming hysterically. As he approached me, I put out my hands saying that I was "peaceful and he could take me away - I've made my point." At this moment the security guard flung his arms in the air and ran away yelling and shouting to his colleagues by the van. They too started yelling and shouting, then I heard sirens approaching. It was then, I admit, I lost it in the head a little. This had never happened before whether at protests or on the football field - it was probably a mixture of exhaustion and stress at the situation. We all make mistakes occasionally. I then started pulling the crops and after I'd picked a few - about a quarter of a fertiliser bag, walked over to the police who were entering the field.

The security were still panicking, but the police could see I was not a danger and didn't bother putting me in handcuffs. As we left the site in the police car, we passed groups of 5 or 6 police cars. I asked, quite innocently, if there was another crime being committed round here at the same time. They said no and that this was all due to me. Even with this, I didn't think what I'd done was that bad and it was just a huge overreaction. This was born out when the police asked if I wanted a Solicitor to which I said I was sure that wouldn't be necessary.

We were on our way to Harpenden Police Station, but then were re-directed to Stevenage for some reason (probably because they had more 'resources' at Stevenage). On arrival I had my fingerprints, photograph and DNA taken then popped into a cell. (They were amazed I'd got away without doing this until now with my chequered past)I asked if I could have my book 'The Power of Now' by Eckhart Tolle, but was told I couldn't have it. Instead they gave me 3 magazines the likes of which my daughter had given up on by the time she was 15 - staring at the wall was less torturous than reading about the lives of Simon Cowell and Jordan's latest breast implant CONCERNS.

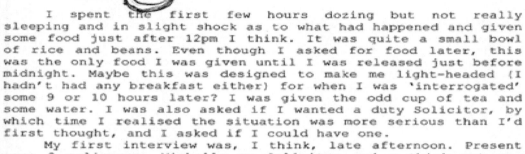

I spent the first few hours dozing but not really sleeping and in slight shock as to what had happened and given some food just after 12pm I think. It was quite a small bowl of rice and beans. Even though I asked for food later, this was the only food I was given until I was released just before midnight. Maybe this was designed to make me light-headed (I hadn't had any breakfast either) for when I was 'interrogated' some 9 or 10 hours later? I was given the odd cup of tea and some water. I was also asked if I wanted a duty Solicitor, by which time I realised the situation was more serious than I'd first thought, and I asked if I could have one.

My first interview was, I think, late afternoon. Present were 2 policemen, Michelle my Solicitor and a thick set guy with short silver hair who sat behind me throughout the proceedings (and I was to see later). I was told that the reason everything was taking so long was because they were busy processing a lot of people from the night before (yet I was one of 2 other people max in the cells), and "they were waiting for someone to 'help' me to come up from London?"

My Solicitor advised me to say 'no comment' to everything other than my name, but I felt bad about doing that and did answer most of the questions. After this I was put back in the cell for a few more hours and resigned to be there overnight. Then the door opened and there were 2 tall plain clothes fellows (one being the guy sitting behind me during the first interview), who asked if I would go and have a chat with them. Not knowing the protocol, bored (my celeb magazines had been replaced with "Good Housekeeping 2008") I went with them.

I was taken into an interrogation room and the guy I hadn't met came over all pally pally. He said he'd "just like a friendly chat . . . .I'm a big admirer of yours and I'd like to get to know the real Hector and what makes you tick." He also said that he had no tapes and it was all informal.

After a lot of buttering up the questions became less friendly. They wanted me to tell them about which organisations I was working with and wanting names of people and future plans. I pointed out that the situation was becoming less friendly, to which he kept saying "Hector I really like and admire you, I just want to get to know you." I stressed that I was a loner and would join in with others if I believed their gripe was right. The only group I mentioned was Climate Camp because they have now ceased. But it made no odds because he knew all about Globalise Resistance, the names of my friends in the movement, practically every demo I'd ever been on from Gleneagles to anti-war protests and so on.

He was also familiar with the 2 books I've written and quoted from the second one that 'we must fight tirelessly to bring down capitalism in its current guise in any and every way we can . . .' I told him it's 'just a book' to start with and written 9 odd years ago when I was raw and new to protesting etc.

Last but not least he produced the photos in my bag which a colleague had sent to give me a clue as to where the site was. I told him it was no damn good to me because the map was tiny and had no writing on it. He then pointed out 2 random photos. One of the photos being of the Rothampstead Research building itself, the other a close up of a number plate. I hadn't registered these pictures because I was only interested in the site. He then became quite intense about what we intended to do with the car and its owner, and I asked him "is this what this whole interrogation is about?" I told him the truth — that I could see how this could be perceived to be a bit suss and said did he think I would ever work or even associate myself with any person/body who planned to target another person with any sort of aggression? This is totally true — I'm a pacifist who simply cares, maybe too much at times, but we are what we are. I'm sure this was just a random photo maybe of a Monsanto boss taken for the sake of it.

I was popped back in the cell, shaken by the grilling and wondering what they had in store for me next. They let me out soon afterwards and fortunately hadn't crushed my car as the guy with short grey hair had repeatedly told me they would. However, it didn't stop there as they insisted I drove all the way back to Devon that night. I told them that it could be dangerous for me and others on the road because I was so tired, plus I had to pick up my dog in Berkshire en route. They told me 'they'd pick me up' if I didn't go back to Devon and 'expect to see the odd police car.' I'm sure they've bugged my car with a bleeper or something, plus they've taken my book 'The Power of Now' and a new set of fencing pliers which I stress were not in my rucksack when I set off but under my car seat. What are the chances of getting these back? I very nearly did crash on the way home and got back just before 6am

I have decided to represent myself at the Magistrates Court in St. Albans Herts on Friday 13th July at 9.0am. I will pay a fine (if that's what is decided) but will refuse if I believe it is extortionate. They feel I have done £3,800 worth of damage — a figure plucked out of the air, but low enough to keep it under the £5,000 threshold when I would have been tried by a Judge and Jury who, I've been told, would have been more sympathetic to a political argument. This to pave the way for a (I believe) fairer, better world.

This for the record, is my last protest — Capitalism looks more than equipped than ever to blow itself to pieces once and for all.

Last but not least, in last week's G2 section of the Guardian on 23.5.12 there was a healthy debate on the pros and cons of GM in the lead-up to the demonstration on May 27th. Pro-GM Chairman of the British Crop Production Council, Colin Ruscoe in his last blast at we anti-GM 'luddites' states in the final paragraph: 'However, whether the protesters like it or not, GM crops are already heading towards Europe. Eventually, due to their use in neighbouring regions, we will get GM crops blowing into Europe over borders. There will be leaks in the dyke. We need to accept and prepare for this, not fear it'. Over my dead body . . . .

SUMMARY

'Innocent' until PROVEN 'guilty' . . . . .was a phase I've been brought up with and, like most people I'm sure, believe is one of the important bedrocks of our Democracy.

At each court hearing the Prosecution were asked : a to produce the 5 to 600 plants I'd "uprooted" according to Huw Dylan Jones' 4 page witness statement (Mr Jones states he is "a plant molecular geneticist and is employed by Rothampstead.)"

Mr. Jones also states that "the field experiment is funded by the RBSRC - the Biotech Industry." This when it's been publicly stated so far that the trial was Government sponsored.

The 500 - 600 plants Mr. Jones states 'I uprooted' were not submitted at any of my hearings (hence I've only paid for the 2-3 max pulled). Mr. Jones states he has the 'evidence' in a deep freeze weighing in at "1.6kg frozen, 1.29kg unfrozen." Believe me, 550 odd plants would weigh a darn site more than this. This figure equates to the plants I pulled and leaf pulled from different plants which would have ALL grown back and recovered when the rains came 10 days later.

In addition to this we requested details of correspondence between the relevant police, Home office, BBSRC, Rothampstead etc regarding the value of the damage and how the valuation leapt from £3,800 to £51,900 as I was entering the court room (after a 6 hour wait . . . . I wonder if the ITN Central News van parked outside the courtroom all day had something to do with this - it seems certain that they are doing all they can to slip GM into this country as under the radar as they can).

The CCTV footage of events we asked for was also not forthcoming. This would have shown me peacefully offering myself to Rana Farood (the security guard) after I'd spread a bit of organic wheat seed - I had absolutely NO intention of pulling plants when I got in. I'm not a vandal. Mr. Farood conveniently left this précis out of his submission.

Add to this the intimidating treatment at Stevenage Police Station - one small meal in 16 hours, little water, 2 interrogations with unsettling lies . . . "your car has been crushed as is practice in such extreme crimes . ."

I pleaded 'guilty' at my last hearing after 3 months because I'd burnt out. I'm guilty of trespass and minor damage, but they have made me feel like a major criminal.

Until very recently, I have not been 100% sure of the real toxicity of Roundup. However recently I have read the findings of Frederique Baudouin published in the high ranked Scientific Journal "Toxicology" about safety studies on Roundup which stated " the health and environmental agencies and pesticide companies assess the long-term effects on mammals of GLYPHOSATE (an ingredient of "Roundup" – the less toxic compound) ALONE. However, the complex mix contains added ingredients – ADJUVANTS. These are classified as INERT but without these the glyphosate would not be stabilised enough to help penetrate the thick (cellular) walls (i.e. without this Roundup wouldn't work). . . . the health and environmental agencies and pesticide companies assess the long-term effects in mammals of GLYPHOSATE ALONE. . . "

This gave me 99% confirmation, but I'm one of those people who doesn't just believe anything I hear or read. I need confirmation from a reputable source/expert in this field if I'm to act on anything. This I received on 7.10.14 while sharing a platform with Vandana Shiva, a well respected expert on GM, at Dartington Hall, Totnes. I asked her if the above was true, and she said "Yes . . . the surfacnt POAE's (adjuvants) are a powerful carcinogen/endocrine disrupter . . . it is true they test glyphosate on its own . . . the EFSA simply accept Monsanto's word it's safe." Being a farmer, I remember when I was freely spraying Roundup (not for a few years) I never wore a mask because I was told "Roundup is one of the safest herbicides on the market". We now hear it's in people's urine and women's breast milk and in 86% of all non organic bread found in supermarkets.

15 May 2014

Mr Michael Meacher MP
House of Commons
London SW1A 0AA

Dear Mr Meacher

On 12 May you tabled a named day PQ to the House of Commons Commission for answer today, Thursday 15 May. As prorogation occurred yesterday the question has fallen; however, a response was prepared and may be of use to you.

You asked whether GM food is sold in restaurants and bars in the House. Catering Services GM policy prohibits the purchase of GM foods. This is not on ethical or environmental grounds, but reflects current public views on the subject as reflected in the trade press. The policy states that, while evidence and advice from scientific and governmental bodies and indeed the wider food industry is generally taken into account, the decision to avoid GM products has been enforced as a matter of customer choice, based on our understanding of the wider public's view on the issue.

We hope this answer

Yours sincerely

Robert Twigger
Secretary of the Commission

House of Commons Commission House of Commons London SW1A 0AA
T: 020 7219 3270 F: 020 7219 2622 E: twiggerrj@parliament.uk

TAKE BACK THE FLOUR PART 2

"GMO'S THE FINAL CURTAIN CALL"

I don't know about you but I personally have had enough of the world's largest corporations controlling our Government and deciding 'our future' (with the notable exception of Russia).

Since 2012 I have been banned from Hertfordshire because I scaled the fence protecting the GM wheat trial and, as can be seen from the enclosed, been 'blessed' enough to have had a 'visit' or 2 since then. I've also found out I'm still banned from Hertfordshire 6 years later as this has upset my insurance company.

Enclosed is a bit of background: I've been involved and sometimes organising events in the UK and across Europe raising concerns about the health of our pesticide-ridden foods and the world's favourite herbicide Roundup. Since the ban (I'd love to know how many other people have been banned from a county out of curiosity.). I've been to Rothamstead Research Centre a few times and the 'field' (where I took a host of pictures under an untold number of security cameras over a 2 hour period undetected where I visualised I had an 'INVISIBLE cloak'- odd though it seems, this DOES work . . .)

The 'package' gives more examples of this and I can promise you it's all true and I believe . . .(and I don't care how dotty I sound — too much evidence) there are more angels than ever ready to help, but they can ONLY help if we make ourselves 'available' to them and by that I mean 'following the song of our hearts without Fear . . .'

We have a date set for August 15th. Please come and bring your friends. It will be a non-violent yet colourful Direct Action. We will meet at 1pm in Harpenden at the "Inn on the Green, 20 Leyton Road". We will then walk down to the 'Pods' as I call them (the science labs and offices etc) of the BBSRC (the Research Centre). Here we will create a colourful demonstration with the objective being to politely engage with senior staff and scientists to convince us that the Genetic Modification of this or that are safe for 'we' the public to eat. The same for sprays — as per the ubiquitously used 'Roundup' and any other pesticides for that matter.

Following this I suggest we drive a couple of miles down the road (with a few journalists at foot) and do a small, civilised but highly focussed demonstration around the (now) 2 tiered fence. Here we will demand long term independent testing to find out if consuming GM products (and their favourite 'sidekick' Roundup) are safe for us to eat and feed our animals.

LOVE AND PEACE

INFO FOR THE PUBLIC

Should we be wary of feeding ourselves and/or our children and pets (yes it's in most dog food - unlabelled) food derived from Genetically modified (GM) crops?

What's wrong with inserting a flounder gene into a tomato plant so tomatoes can be grown 200 miles further North, or a synthetic cow gene into a wheat plant to repel aphids?

Why don't those anti-science, ignorant, luddites shut up and let the well qualified experts do their job?

How else will we feed the world?

- We ALL of us have no problem with any of the above provided long-term independent feeding trials have been done to prove GM food is safe for us to eat/feed our children AND safe for the environment i.e. will not cross pollinate with conventional or organic crops. If only . . . . .
- In the late 1990's Government scientist Dr. Arpad Puztai was employed to do experiments on rats fed GM potatoes and non-GM potatoes. He found problems in the rats fed GM compared to those fed non-GM potatoes. Then after he published his results in a Scientific Journal the men in black descended confiscating his computers and evidence and Putzai fled in fear of his life to Eastern Europe.
- Likewise in 2013 when Dr Seralini, a bonifide French scientist, did the first proper long-term survey on rats fed GM compared to those not fed GM. It was (incredibly) the first EVER trial over a 2 year period (90 days, as was the standard length before this, is not long enough). He found up to 80% of rats fed GM got huge tumours compared to 20% fed normal food

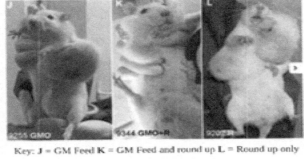

Key: J = GM Feed K = GM Feed and round up L = Round up only

Scientists that fed GM soya and maize to rats found that up to **80% developed huge tumours.**

- Government (for that read 'Biotech' we're afraid) scientists, did all they could to discredit Seralini's findings - the best they came up with was Seralini didn't use enough rats (10 per sample).
- You would have thought if our Government genuinely cared for those it was governing it would have said 'crickey, maybe it's time we got scientist from both sides to come together, agree on a methodology and, in the name of humanity, do proper long-term testing to ascertain once and for all the safety or otherwise of GM?
- "Why on earth does this not happen" I hear rational people with a heart ask?
- ALL recent Environment Ministers since 2001 have, it so obviously seems, been selected for their pro-GM stance . . . Owen Patterson is so aggressively in favour of farmers the world over - including the UK growing GM, it's scary.

Watch:
www.GMcropsfarmertofarmer.com
Remember:
Only WE can STOP GM
Contact: gm@caerhys.co.uk

ROUNDUP –

1.   As I understand it, and I am very happy to be 'corrected', Roundup is a mixture made up of glyphosate and 'additives' known as adjuvants, surfactants or POEA's. Glyphosate is the active ingredient that 'kills' the plants – roots and all, but it needs those adjuvants to break down the fibrous cellular walls/open the pores to allow the glyphosate in.

The Adjuvants 'can' be made up of pretty harmless/inert substances such as animal fat. The problem comes when the 2 (or more) are mixed together in the 'formulation' which often results in a 'synergistic' effect which means the combined effect of the two chemicals are much greater than the sum of the effects of each agent given alone.

In 1999 a German forestry worker was 'poisoned'. He developed chest pains with rapidly increasing respiratory distress and a fever up to 38°. His pathology revealed "toxic inflammation of the lungs that was significantly different from bacterial infection." He'd been spraying Roundup and, following thorough tests, it was found that this was a direct result of the Roundup and the much used surfacant POEA. Added to this, researchers found that adjuvants in Roundup changed the permeability of human cells which further amplfies the toxicity of glyphosate.

ALL DAMAGE VISIBLE...

The result is Germany, which has 91 registered products (of glyphosate), has now banned ALL POEA surfacants. In stark contrast we in the UK have 424 glyphosate products. No-one knows how many contain POEA - and our Government clearly doesn't care/isn't bothered about finding out. I'm afraid it's yet again the old adage of 'Profit before people/cloak and dagger politics'.

Much of this information is available ('buried . .')in a chapter of a 'book' comprising more than 5000 pages of which my bull terrier of a colleague,Pete,who after doggedly reading it, described it as 'deliberately the most boring piece of writing ever written to try to guarantee no-one would bother to read it'. The German Environmental body, the BFR, responsible for Risk Assessment (RA), is the ONLY body in Europe who seem to actually care about our health - acutely aware of the serious problems of 'Formulations/Mixes of substances inert or active', rather than simply testing each product on its own.

In the US, due to a build up of resistance of weeds and pests from using the same herbicide (roundup) and pesticide (BT toxin) for years, combined with monoculture agriculture (we rightly have to rotate our crops in the UK to help us to at least reduce pesticide use), the weeds and bugs have effectively 'Genetically Modified' themselves. The resulting 'resistance' has meant up to 5 applications of Roundup a year, AND patented (which means anyone caught copying it will be prosecuted) tank mixes of Roundup, Atrazine and 2-4D .The latter two are currently both banned in Europe, for 'health reasons' - 2-4D being a product very similar in make up to Monsanto's 'favourite' WMD 'Agent Orange' which is frequently sprayed from the air in South America 'drifting' in and around local communities.

Roundup was originally designed to be purely a pre-emergent weed killer. This means it is sprayed onto the ground before the seed is sown to kill all weeds and to give the crop a good chance to get going. However, now, due to the build up of resistance (to Roundup)of the weeds, up to 5 applications are sprayed each year. This means 4 applications go directly onto/into the growing crop itself, and through that, of course, into us and our children's bodies, animal feed and pet foods. Some US and Canadian farmers even apply the LAST application of Roundup just 2 days before harvest - this to dessicate (kill) any remaining greenery which prevents some grain being harvested, thus getting a slightly higher yield. It also gives virtually no time for any of the Roundup to be washed away .....

The 'precautionary principle', of basically 'safe until proved otherwise', is nothing but a thorn in the side of these huge multinational companies. ALL agriculture Ministers since Michael Meacher was sacked in June 2003 by Blair - because he cared about the environment and declared his findings honestly, have been specially selected for their pro-GM stance.

Recent Biotech trained environment Ministers have included Caroline Spelman who, along with her husband, worked for the Biotech industry (amongst other things) beforehand for, I believe, 16 years. Then there was Owen Patterson who was so aggressively pro-GM and openly hostile about all campaigners (especially me when I got into the GM wheat trials at Rothampstead, Hertfordshire - a county from which I am 'banned' where I scattered organic wheat seed and pulled plants).

Now we have Liz Truss who to us, like Caroline Spelman, is a far more dangerous prospect than Patterson who was like a bull in a china shop where all he did was break an awful lot of china. She broke her silence on GM after 6 months in office at the Oxford Farming Conference. 4 times the number of people were down the road at the same time at the 'The Oxford "Real" Farming Conference' discussing sustainable, chemical free agriculture without GM crops when Liz Truss announced the green light for GM crops to be grown in this country.

With lobbyists paying small fortunes to wine, dine and have the ear of senior politicians, and our own advisory council of scientists-ACRE comprising a majority of people with 'interests' in the Biotech industry the last time I looked, and it's easy to think 'what hope do we have . . .?' and simply give up as so many of my fellow campaigners have.

However . . .things are changing and more and more facts are surfacing. Tests done in the US on humans and animals found

.e farmers replaced feed for their animals containing GM with conventionally (GM free) grown feed, they said, started to improve after just three days. I have been saying for ages that why can't US, UK and other Governments get together and agree 'in the name of humanity', to get together scientists from both sides of the (cavernous - sadly) divide and agree on a methodology to prove whether GM is safe for us to eat and feed our animals or not. Once we all 'know' whether putting a cow gene into a wheat plant, for example, is safe or not with FULL TRANSPARENCY of how the tests were conducted, no-one will be able to argue, and us, so called 'activists', can then happily get on tending to our veg/permaculture gardens etc (which I'd like to see the whole country covered in - another story).

It hasn't helped that when Government and/or independent scientists such as Dr. Arpad Puztai and Dr. Seralini respectively, release their results they put their lives at serious risk. In the case of Puztai, the day after his results were published, the 'men in black' descended, confiscated all his computers/material and Puztai fled to Hungary in fear for his life. Last year I went up to see Dr. Seralini speak at the Houses of Parliament. Seralini had just completed the first ever test at Caen University in France over a 2 year period on rats. Using the correct scientifically approved methodology for testing he unearthed some worrying results - the longest period of testing before this was 90 days which in the life of a rat, with an average lifespan of $2\frac{1}{2}$ years, is not long enough to produce any conclusive evidence.

Our Houses of Parliament were to be the first port of call for Dr. Seralini who was booked in to do a nationwide tour to farming communities across the UK. Instead Seralini left Parliament on a drip and spent the next 14 days in intensive care fighting for his life. A close friend, ▮▮▮▮▮ and fellow activist against GMO's said that Seralini had 'commented' about someone in the street rubbing something on his bare leg the day before and if ▮▮▮▮ hadn't managed to get his children over (who due to his passion in the laboratory, he hadn't seen for a few years) Seralini might well have not made it. The groundbreaking nationwide tour was, inevitably, cancelled. In a much less dramatic way (thankfully) I was warned by seasoned activists that my life was in danger after highlighting the huge potential danger of GM wheat to our native grass species, health and so on.

If anyone is struggling to accept this you only have to look at the evidence produced by Peter Kindersley at Sheepdrove.com. Here he demonstrates via a series of graphs how incidences of diabetes (age adjusted), liver and intrahepatic bile duct cancer, thyroid cancer, diabetes, senile dementia, Parkinson's and more besides escalated exponentially in 1996

when GM (combined with an accompanying increase in Roundup) was carpet bombed across the USA and Canada.

If anyone reading this finds this hard to believe (and boy I don't blame anyone who does . . .) you only have to go on the net to see how the goalposts have dramatically moved over the last few decades to SOLELY suit the interests of some of the world's largest corporations above all else.

In EXACTLY the same way maximum residue levels (MRL) permitted in food and feed products were raised 200 times to levels previously permitted at the same time GM soya crops were approved. The same has happened with the pharmaceutical companies. One example . . The horrific George Bush's side kick Donald Rumsfeld invested in the Ramazzini Foundation which brought(amongst many other such horrors) Aspartame onto the market. Aspartame is in most soft drinks and one of many 'approved' products on the market with vicious side effects such as MS, muscle spasms, liver failure, autism, Parkinsons disease, depression, brain damage etc etc - even Doctors have referred to such symptoms as 'Rumsfeld Disease'.

The more you dig the more you find out that ALL these huge companies are solely motivated by competing with each other - paying lawyers fortunes to find loopholes in anything they can to lure in investment to service the huge egos of fat cat businessmen. If WE collectively don't say NO to GM, pharmaceuticals, fracking, chemical foods NOW, our children and theirs will not have a world fit to live in. As I always say, if anyone can prove me wrong on any of this, I'll happily hold my hand up and shut up - if not I won't.

There is now, at last, a crescendo of noise from all sorts of bodies and Governments that could, I believe, quickly go from a 'wind of change/increase in awareness' to a full blown hurricane. The World Health Organisation (WHO) recently described Roundup as a 'probable carcinogen.' Russia on the back of Seralini's work, has banned farmers from growing GM crops AND all GM imports for at least 10 years. Likewise, Holland and France will ban Roundup from all garden centres at the end of this year. Interestingly they've not said about banning it in agriculture . . . .This is currently difficult because Monsanto etc have captured the whole market, but many of us, including Zac Goldsmith are experimenting with novel eco-weed killers while others are looking into 'steam', special tines on tractors and so on. Will give up-date as ideas come in. In the meantime please pull (or accept) weeds.

2. Also any advice about alternatives to weed killers like Roundup re this letter I received from a farmer's daughter- Holly. Please see attachment letter.
Thank you
Hector.

Monday, September 21, 20:0
by
Independent Science News

Bill Gates' Global Agenda and How We Can Resist His War on Life

Gates' 'funding' results in an erasure of democracy and biodiversity, of nature and culture. His 'philanthropy' is not just philanthrocapitalism. It is philanthroimperialism.

by
Vandana Shiva

As I look to the future in a world of Gates and Tech Barons, I see a humanity that is further polarized into large numbers of 'throw away' people who have no place in the new Empire.(Photo by Mike Cohen/Getty Images for The New York Times)

In March 2015, Bill Gates showed an image of the coronavirus during a TED Talk and told the audience that it was what the greatest catastrophe of our time would look like. The real threat to life, he said, is 'not missiles, but microbes.' When the coronavirus pandemic swept over the earth like a tsunami five years later, he revived the war language, describing the pandemic as 'a world war'.

'The coronavirus pandemic pits all of humanity against the virus,' he said.

In fact, the pandemic is not a war. The pandemic is a consequence of war. A war against life. The mechanical mind connected to the money machine of extraction has created the illusion of humans as separate from nature, and nature as dead, inert raw material to be exploited. But, in fact, we are part of the biome. And we are part of the virome. The biome and the virome are us. When we wage war on the biodiversity of our forests, our farms, and in our guts, we wage war on ourselves.

The health emergency of the coronavirus is inseparable from the health emergency of extinction, the health emergency of biodiversity loss, and the health emergency of the climate crisis. All of these emergencies are rooted in a mechanistic, militaristic, anthropocentric worldview that considers humans separate from—and superior to—other beings. Beings we can own, manipulate, and control. All of these emergencies are rooted in an economic model based on the illusion of limitless growth and limitless greed, which violate planetary boundaries and destroy the integrity of ecosystems and individual species.

We stand at a precipice of extinction. Will we allow our humanity as living, conscious, intelligent, autonomous beings to be extinguished by a greed machine that does not know limits and is unable to put a brake on its colonization and destruction?

Poisoned

It's taken me 8 months or so to pluck up the courage to write down what happened to me — my stomach churns and I feel sick every time I think about it. I believe there are some extremely nasty people who are paid whatever it takes to protect the interests of the world's biggest Corporations.

It's no secret that I've been on Monsanto's back since 2001 when, after 8 months of fighting to stop the mindless 'culling' of my and other's perfectly healthy cattle, sheep etc, anti GMO Activists persuaded me to join their cause. I'm an all or nothing type and, before I knew it, was going on endless demos across Europe — getting arrested dressed as a GM potato in Germany, heckling Prime Minister Blair(the worst)at the Labour party conference, and Gordon Brown at the G8 in Edinburgh, culminating in vandalising Monsanto's GM wheat trial in 2012 where I got a lifelong ban from Hertfordshire

Last year I had a meeting with anti GMO activists. We felt 'yes' we'd delayed the commercial growing of GM but it's not going to go away unless we get radicle. With the Green Gathering looming in early August and the Off Grid Festival at Tapeley (for the first time – a great honour) and the ground was as fertile as it possibly could be . . . .

The Green Gathering 2ⁿᵈ – 5ᵗʰ August where I've done talks with my comrades ▓▓▓▓▓ and ▓▓▓ for the last 6 years; was our first good opportunity to recruit trusted Activists. Hot on the heels, as mentioned, was the Off Grid Festival where everything imploded in on itself with devastating consequences. . . .

I had planned two very different demonstrations. One was going to be a largish contingent of peaceful activists whereby we'd have between 30-50 people meeting in Harpenden Herts on (private)land belonging to wealthy business folk. Having demonstrated there we planned to march to the new GM wheat trial plots half a mile outside Harpenden itself (where I'd recently paid a private visit 2 or 3 weeks earlier where I'd taken lots of photos – of the now heavily reinforced double fence). This peaceful demonstration was to be on August 15ᵗʰ meeting in Harpenden, Herts at 2pm.

August 24ᵗʰ was our chosen time to then put everything on the line . . . Over this period I'd got together 10 or so trusted friends. Exasperated and angry with more evidence than ever that GMO's and that (ubiquitous) wretched Roundup was killing millions across the world, I bought a load of jerry cans which I filled with petrol which we were simply going to pour upwind of the now 'double fence' (the second fence being built as a direct result of my 2012 action) and chuck a match on it. This would of course have guaranteed me a long prison sentence and possible life had the fire got out of control (remember the ground was tinder dry back then). I swear I was fully prepared for the consequences.

MY DOCUMENT OF EVENTS
By
HECTOR CHRISTIE

It's 6am on Monday morning. I've not slept at all for 2 nights, and drove down from Stevenage Police Station to North Devon as part of my 'condition for bail' narrowly avoiding falling asleep at the wheel. I'm writing this now knowing I won't be able to go to sleep.

Being near to London on Saturday night and with a 'free' Sunday I decided to go to Harpenden, Herts, where Rothampstead research Centre are doing a trial of GM wheat. GM wheat is potentially the most 'dangerous' of all agricultural crops being that the pollen could cross-contaminate our wild native grass species with goodness knows what consequences. It also uses a synthetic gene most similar to that found in a cow. inserted to repel aphids. This when there have been no long term independent tests done to see if this is safe for us to eat or not, plus there are many natural ways to repel aphids. Even the US, Canada and Australia (all GM growers) have refused GM wheat because other countries don't want it and there is no market for it.

I left at 3am Sunday morning with no idea where the site was and searched much of Rothampstead Park starting at dawn. At 6ish I drove to the other side of town and on driving down a side road was confronted with a huge CCTV camera and warnings to trespassers. It was pretty obvious I was in the vicinity. Here I went for a wander and eventually saw the big green fence way off the beaten track.

I'd dressed as a slightly nerdy twitcher to try not to draw attention to myself - with flat cap borrowed from my brother and rather snazzy anorak with go fast lines on it (the sort of thing a rather out of condition person may wear to try to portray the opposite). I also had toy binoculars which I'd put to my eyes scouring treetops for wildlife to put security, watching CCTV, at ease. I deliberately parked underneath a huge security camera for the same reason.

I went back to my car passing a group of 10 or so security guards having a chat by another CCTV camera and pretty much gave up all hope of reaching the site, let alone entering it. I drove down a road following my nose and parked at the rugby club to have a look over one of the few gates that didn't have a trespassers warning sign on it.

I have been on a lot of protests since the appalling foot and mouth - when I was 'activated' (for want of a better word) against the appalling behaviour of so many Big, Corporate Businesses, with the full backing of whatever Government.

I have never done anything subversive or damaging and (rightly or wrongly) didn't consider chucking a few

handfuls of organic wheat onto (what I consider) the potentially polluting GM wheat, a big deal. It was, in my mind, what is considered a fluffy action (in protest terminology) and as such designed to draw more public and media attention to the dangerous situation unfolding in this country.

My reasons for going to Rothampstead Research Centre, Herts to shed the light on the possible consequences from the GM wheat trial being held there.

I must start by saying that I have apologised to fellow activists for going in a week early. I misinterpreted the brief for the day stating that . . 'any further actions were down to individuals themselves.'

With the National Press now largely backing the introduction of GM crops, it's looking ever more likely that the Government will give in under the sustained pressure from some of the world's largest and most powerful corporations.

I feel sad that the Rothampstead Agricultural Research Centre, who have done some wonderful work in the enhancement and increase of production via hybridisation and general conventional methods, have chosen to take up the GM mantle.

The line used by the CEO of Rothampstead was basically that if we don't embrace this technology we will simply not be able to feed the expanding world population likely to reach 9 billion by 2050. If I knew little about the subject and had even been against it in the past, I would get won over by this simple point on its own and 'to hell with the rest of it.'

Sadly this information we are being fed is a lie of the highest order.

I strongly urge everybody to watch a short documentary on the net called GMcropsfarmertofarmer.com. The ½ hour program is akin to a 'survey' done by a Cornish farmer interviewing US farmers on how growing GM crops has affected their livelihoods. This is something you'd have thought our Government would have done before going down this route.

PLEASE COME TO THE CAMPAIGN'S TENT

SUNDAY NOON

HECTOR CHRISTIE, JIM McNULTY AND WELSH LEGEND
GERALD MILES

ROTHAMSTEAD RESEARCH CENTRE HERTS
-THE BATTLEGROUND OF GMO/ROUNDUP
ACTIVISM - WITH 'SINGALONG' . . .
CAMPAIGN'S TENT 12PM SUNDAY

Anti-GMO activist found dead in hotel pool, hours before planned delivery of 200,000 petition signatures to the EPA

naturalnews.com/2018-04-13-anti-gmo-activist-found-dead-in-hotel-pool-hours-before-planned-delivery-of-200000-petition-signatures-to-the-epa.html
Mike Adams

April 13, 2018

(Natural News) An activist who opposed genetically engineered mosquitoes has been found dead in the swimming pool of a Washington D.C. hotel, just hours before she was due to submit a petition with over 200,000 signatures to the EPA.

Derrick Broze of Activist Post has investigated the story and spoken to a close friend of the victim, whose name is Mila de Mier from Key West, Florida (see below).

The mysterious death has also been covered by WJLA, which reports:

The D.C. Fire Department says the reported incident happened at the Cambria Hotel & Suites Washington, D.C. Convention Center on 899 O Street, NW. They say they were called to the scene at around 9:35 a.m. Medical crews say they attempted to treat the victim but later pronounced her dead.

Her death, of course, reminds informed observers of all the death threats that other anti-GMO activists have been subjected to over the years, thanks to the "black ops" biotech industry running intimidation campaigns, reputation smear campaigns and political bribery campaigns to grease the palms of politicians. If you weren't aware that people who oppose the biotech giants or vaccine industry are being **routinely assassinated across America**, you're not up to speed on what's really happening.

advocating GM is now saying that we must revert to large scale, intensive pig, cattle and poultry farming to meet the shortfall (at around 40% I believe), of our own needs in the UK. As this world teeters ever closer to the brink he is right to try to address this issue. However, the appalling beyond belief --- welfare issues aside, do we want to put yet more of our eggs in the Corporate (farming) basket or is there another way?

Agricultural writers and author of several books on the countryside, Graham Harvey states that: "the truth is that there's now a consensus of farm scientists who believe the planet is quite capable of feeding a population of nine billion using present knowledge and methods (IAASTD report, 2008). That's so long as we don't continue to wreck our soils using the current pesticide-dependent wheat growing methods of Britain and America.

The reason so many research resources are being squandered on GM technology is that back in the early 1980's the then funding authority - the Agricultural Research Council - identified genetic manipulation as a priority area. As a result of this decision we now have a generation of research scientist who've built their careers on this narrow and largely pointless technology."

As can be seen on GMcropsfarmertofarmer.com, in vast areas of the States it is impossible to buy conventional seed anymore - such is the control and dominance of Monsanto. The excellent scientists who would have been working on improving yields and disease resistance, have mostly been 'persuaded' to work for the large GM conglomerates.

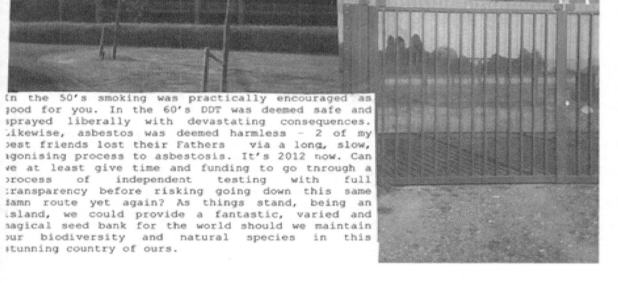

In the 50's smoking was practically encouraged as good for you. In the 60's DDT was deemed safe and sprayed liberally with devastating consequences. Likewise, asbestos was deemed harmless - 2 of my best friends lost their Fathers via a long, slow, agonising process to asbestosis. It's 2012 now. Can we at least give time and funding to go through a process of independent testing with full transparency before risking going down this same damn route yet again? As things stand, being an island, we could provide a fantastic, varied and magical seed bank for the world should we maintain our biodiversity and natural species in this stunning country of ours.

Dear Toby. I'm potentially coming up your way next week or the week after – I'm making a lot of trips currently to see my dear old Mum. I seem to remember last year that you said you might be able to show me and another around the site and what you're doing which you said could allay some of our fears. Obviously we're very disappointed that Roundup/Glyphosate ('probably' carcinogenic as they say now) has been granted a new licence for at least another 5 years. Please could you call me with some dates that could suit you. With best wishes, Hector

Thursday 26th April 2018- tobyjabruce@gmail.com

Dear Hector.

I'm no longer employed at Rothamstead and work in a different part of the country (Keele University). I can ask my former colleagues if they can arrange a tour for you if you like?

Although no longer there, I do miss the place. I have great admiration for the valiant research efforts Rothamstead makes to advance agriculture for the benefit of humanity as a public sector (non-profit) organisation. I guess you think it is an ethical position to oppose GM crops and use of any non-natural chemicals in food production. PLEASE MAY I BE SO BOLD AS TO CHALLENGE THE THINKING BEHIND THAT – IS IT ETHICAL TO IMPOSE RESTRICTIONS ON THE REST OF HUMANITY INCLUDING THOSE IN A MUCH LESS FORTUNATE SITUATION THAN YOU ARE IN? I know food security is a complicated and multi-faceted thing but I do believe public sector organisations working to advance agriculture are part of the solution not part of the problem or something to be feared.

Best wishes,

Toby.

This demonstration will be a precursor to the big one – "DECONTAMINATE THE CONTAMINATION SITE" at Rothamsted Research Centre on Sunday May 27th (see stopgmo.org. Details of the demonstration will be put on the website closer to the time).

OUR FOOD...NOT YOUR BUSINESS!

Aristocrat activist leads day of action to 'round up the Roundup'

Catherine Early

31st August, 2017

Hector Christie, owner of the Tapeley Park estate and farm in Devon and renowned environmental campaigner, is urging the public to join a day of action against the Roundup weedkiller. CATHERINE EARLY reports

Roundup is a horrendous substance, there is so much evidence out there on its impact on human health. It feels like the right time to do this.

Managers of supermarkets and garden centres might be surprised to see stocks of the weedkiller Roundup vanishing from their shelves next week. The reason will become clear when customers put them on the spot as to why they are stocking the controversial product.

This is the plan for Christie's national day of action on 5 September. Christie's 20 years of campaigning have seen him dressed as vegetables, heckling prime ministers and arrested and charged with criminal damage. He has railed against the slaughter of animals during the Foot and Mouth crisis, the use of genetically modified seeds and the Iraq war. But, he claims that support for his anti-Roundup campaign has been overwhelming and more than he has previously experienced.

Christie will be leading the charge in his local town of Barnstaple, where he plans to stage a protest in every supermarket. The use of the herbicide leaves Christie "quivering with anger", he said. "It's believed to be a carcinogen, it needs to be exposed. Roundup is a horrendous substance, there is so much evidence out there on its impact on human health. It feels like the right time to do this.

Beautiful planet

"Let's roundup the Roundup and banish it - and the companies who make it - from our beautiful planet once and for all," he told The Ecologist.

The controversial weedkiller is in the spotlight again as a crucial decision on its future in Europe is set to be made in the autumn. The European Commission is considering whether to extend the substance's licence. It was originally due to make a decision last year, but instead granted a temporary extension days before the licence expired.

In May, EU health commissioner Vytenis Andriukaitis proposed a ten-year extension to the approval of the herbicide, originally patented by Monsanto for Roundup but now manufactured by some 20 companies.

This Author

Catherine Early is a freelance environmental journalist and the former deputy editor of the environmentalist. She can be found tweeting at @Cat_Early76

MAKE ROUNDUP HISTORY CAMPAIGN

Calling you to participate in a Day of Action against *Roundup*, The Monsanto Toxic Herbicide. 1-2pm, 6th September 2017

Roundup is a Probable Carcinogen, say The World Health Organisation

Roundup is a herbicide used to kill weeds. It is sprayed on our farms, on our food, on wheat just before harvest, and is even sprayed in our playgrounds. It poisons water, the air, our food, our pets, our children and our bodies.

It's time to join the international campaign *Saying No to Roundup!* Take action on 6th September to help remove it from our shop shelves.
Information on how to join the campaign is included at the end of this document

Round Up RoundUp

THE GREAT CORPORATE CON

You've probably noticed when people refer to Monsanto's favourite herbicide they refer to it as either Glyphosate or Roundup implying it's pretty much the same thing. You've all no doubt heard people say that "glyphosate won't 'probably' damage you if you accidently ingest some . . ." This is true BUT what they conveniently leave out is Roundup, in its complete form, also has chemicals added to it known as "inert ingredients."

Sharon Lerner writes that . . . "these (inert ingredients) chemicals have evaded scientific scrutiny and regulation in part because the companies that make and use them have concealed their identity as 'Trade Secrets'. "The 'imaginatively' (literally) named 'polyethoxylated tallowamine' is 'used in Monsanto's Roundup classic original formulations among other weed killers, to aid in penetrating the waxy surface of plants.'

Without these adjuvants/subjuvants which also break down the plants protective cellular wall, glyphosate (on its own) wouldn't work. I find myself quivering with anger as I write this and I feel the need to reign myself in to not do something stupid. Millions are dying each year because of this convoluted misinformation. PLEASE rise up and spread the word about this demo on September 6th and lets bloody well Roundup the Roundup and banish it (and the companies who make it) from our beautiful planet once and for all.

 HECTOR

THREE "BLIND" (GENETICALLY MODIFIED) MICE

Gmo's . . . . .Gmo's
See how they spread
See how they grow
They all ran after the farmer's wife
They damaged her kidneys and took her life
Have you ever known there be so much strife
From Gmo's . . . .Gmo's

OUR NEXT NURSERY RHYME IS CALLED BAA BAA BLACK SHEEP

It's about Dolly's first cousin – Molly. Molly has been cloned to produce 3 times more wool than normal sheep. Even though cloned Mollies suffer acute respiratory problems, have chronic pains in their joints and live half the lifespan of a normal sheep, the economics outweigh all this and Molly's given the commercial green light.

Baa Baa Black sheep
Have you any wool
So friggin much I feel like a fool
I'm cloned and confused, don't know what they've done
Not sure if I'm a Dad or a Mum
Baa Baa Black sheep have you any wool?
Please end my life, then I'll be cool.

Please sign here to put on your 'Green Gloves' and help us pull the little blighters should they be grown (PTO for reasons).

NAME	ADDRESS & E-MAIL	TEL No	Signature

Please get friends to sign up and add a page of more names if you can. Return to Hector Christie, Tapeley Park, Instow, North Devon. EX39 4NT or hector15@btinternet.com. Thank you.

How to join in the campaign

Take just one hour of your day between 1 – 2 pm, on 6th September 2017 to visit any retail outlet, supermarket or farm shop selling Roundup. Take as many people with you as you can muster.

Fill up your trolley with as much Roundup as you can and go to the Check Out or Customer Service.

Ask to see the manager. Ask why their store is selling a product that is considered carcinogenic by the Public Health Organisation, that is poisoning our homes, our parks, our food, our children, our water, our air, our bodies?

Explain why they should be removing Roundup from their shelves, and demand that it be removed from the shelves.

Invite the local press to do a feature and take photos of your 'action' to gain more momentum and wider public awareness of the dangers of Roundup.

A poster and information sheets will be provided to organisers of such actions, to help (those who want it) explain the dangers and consequences of Roundup on our environment and our health.

For more information please contact Campaign Organisers, Hector Christie hector15@btinternet.com or Gerald Miles gm@caerhys.co.uk or Jim McNulty - nonat_is e@yahoo.co.uk

We'd love to know about any actions you take to support this campaign, so please send us any details that you have and stories of how your action went and any photos.

GLYPHOSATE PREC
CAUSES CANCER

29 October 2018

I am currently going through the toughest battle of my life.

A month or so ago I was walking down a street in shorts, in my local town of Bideford, when I felt a rubber glove rub on my exposed thigh – 'filthy pervert' I thought to myself and walked on.

A few days later I was getting hot and cold sweats. That alarmed me as we were due to have the 'OFF GRID' Festival here at Tapeley on the 9-12 August, where I put all my remaining energy into my two talks and making sure everybody was looked after. Thankfully, the good Lord answered my prayers and, à la Moses, parted the Red Sea and staved off the fever / extraordinary pain I had inside me until the Monday morning. That gave me an opportunity to announce, shaking like a leaf/ brimming with emotion, that the Californian, black farmer – the subject of the poisoning, had successfully just won his court case some three hours earlier proving his (now) terminal condition was directly caused by the (unashamedly evil) Monsanto. I said that this would open up the floodgates across the world to farmers and gardeners who spray their patios, parks, children's' play areas etc with Roundup, to sue these horrendously disgusting companies and get people back away from the office and back to the land. Then Theo Simon, the lead singer of my favourite protest band 'Seize the Day', whispered in my ear: "that was the best end to a gig we've ever had....".

I am not the paranoid type at all but have been warned a number of times by fellow compatriots that I really needed to 'watch my back' (whatever the heck that means). I first encountered that when I vandalised the first ever GM wheat trial at Rothamsted Research Centre in 2012 where soon after I was released I was MADE to drive from Hertfordshire to Devon at 1am after three days of no sleep – no doubt in the hope that I would fall asleep at the wheel – where police cars were parked in laybys every 20—30 miles to make sure I went back to Devon and didn't turn around to 'finish off the job'.

███████ the activist I respected above all else, contacted me and said she "really needed to meet up with me", so we arranged to meet at Tiverton Parkway railway station at 1pm. The three police cars in lay-bys and two bobbies in the empty train station making fleeting glances between the train timetable and us, to which I asked politely if I could help them understand which train they needed to catch (?!), prepared me in a way for the next five years of bailiffs, injunctions, uncertainties and threats.

I've recently (reluctantly) paid my fine, this when the London bailiffs got permission to smash my door down and take the William Morris furniture. Normally bailiffs charge the troublemaker for each visit they make but that didn't apply to me. This was because if the fine went past the 5k mark (my fine was £4,300) I'd be entitled to a full jury inclusive of press and they weren't going to allow this for all the tea in China.

I must stress again that every doctor I've seen hasn't got a clue as to why I'm so ill.....so if I have been 'given' something it's totally untraceable. I will keep fighting – as I've always done, but this is getting harder and harder by the day. Wanting my children to have a decent Dad is my main motivating force – B&A have been angelic to me these past few days /weeks (so what more would I want I rightly hear you say...)

Ps Got a numb right foot
Pps No more protests for me
Ppps Need a shave
Pppps Sorry for any incoherence to comprehend – hopefully gives enough – my Spirit is Broken
Ppppps I've lost a stone in a month and still losing weight – need to carve more holes in my belt every other day.

You are shortly to meet with Dr Bourke. The purpose of this meeting will be to allow Dr Bourke to provide you with a diagnosis and a management plan, aimed at improving your current clinical state.

To assist with this, please take the time in advance of your appointment to answer the questions in this document. You need not complete it all at once if you feel that this is too much but it is of great importance that you complete all questions prior to your appointment with Dr Bourke. This provides meaningful information that will assist in finding the optimal course to assist with your recovery.

Many of the questions require a simple yes/no response. However, there is also space provided for you to add a further description.

Please bring the completed document with you to your appointment.

NAME: HECTOR CHRISTIE

DATE: 20/9/18

Do you have a job at the moment? ~~Yes~~ / No

If not, when did you last work and what has been the reason for not working?

Are you currently on sick leave from work?   Yes/No

What was the highest education you achieved? (Please circle)

None   O-level/GCSE   (NVQ   A-level)

Undergraduate   Postgraduate

How many days per week and you working? (Please circle)

(0)   1   2   3   4   5   6   7

What is your job now or your last job since you became unwell?
FARMER

A message to all farmers on the Estate

e-mail hector15@btinternet.com

Dear

I'm really really sorry to be a pain, but, from now on, I don't want Roundup applied to any land on the Estate. I know for you cereal growers especially this could seem like a major inconvenience. If that causes a real problem to any of you over the transition period as you get used to "life without Roundup" please call me and we'll meet to agree the best way forward. We will also look into giving discount rents to those who go organic.

There is now more evidence than ever about the toxic effects of Monsanto's Roundup on the land – damage to beneficial soil micro organisms, wild life etc, watercourses and our own health. This is in no way better summarised than by Dr Mercola's document "Monsanto's Roundup herbicide may be the most important factor in development of Autism and other chronic diseases" 9.6.13 (enclosed)

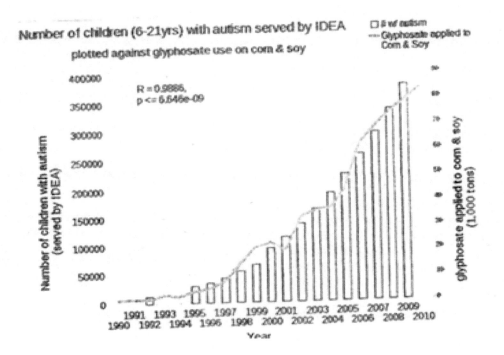

Number of children (6-21yrs) with autism served by IDEA plotted against glyphosate use on corn & soy

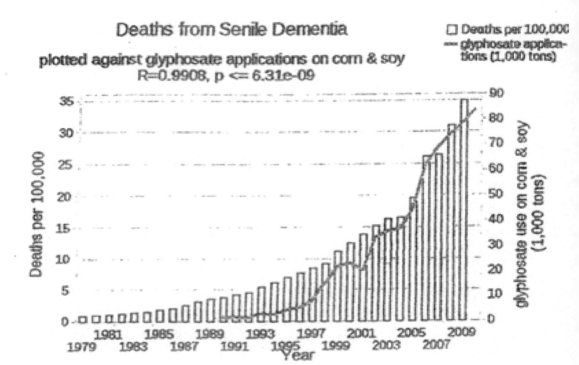

Deaths from Senile Dementia

plotted against glyphosate applications on corn & soy
R=0.9908, p <= 6.31e-09

Legend: □ Deaths per 100,000 — glyphosate applications (1,000 tons)

Acknowledgment: Jon Abrahamson helped with data mining for this article.

Notes:
In 2006 Irena Ermakova reported to the European Congress of Psychiatry that, "As in previous series the behavior of males from GM group was compared with the behavior of control rats. Obtained data showed a high level of anxiety and aggression in males, females and young pups from GM groups. Aggression was more expressed in females and rat pups: they attacked and bite each other and the worker." 14th European Congress of Psychiatry, Nice, France, Sunday, March 5 2006, Poster #048.

Numerous anecdotal reports of animals on GMO diets behaving aggressively and anti-socially have been reported by farmers and veterinarians.

In 2010 Shelton et al. published a paper describing potential mechanisms linking pesticides and autism.

In 2006, Grandjean and Landrigan reported on developmental neurotoxicity of industrial chemicals. "Neurodevelopmental disorders such as autism, attention deficit disorder, mental retardation, and cerebral palsy are common, costly, and can cause lifelong disability. ... Exposure to these chemicals during early fetal development can cause brain injury at doses much lower than those affecting adult brain function."

George Monbiot
7 Ellesmere Road
Oxford OX4 4JG
07890 444271

To: Central West Hertfordshire Magistrates Court,
Civic Centre,
St Peters Street,
St Albans,
AL1 3LB.

Character Reference for Hector Christie
4th July 2012

I am a writer and journalist. I am contracted to the Guardian newspaper, for which I write a weekly column, and to Penguin, for whom I am writing my current book. I am 49 years old (born on 27.01.1963). I am the author of a number of books, including the best-sellers *Heat: how to stop the planet burning* and *The Age of Consent: a manifesto for a new world order*. I have honorary doctorates at the universities of St Andrews and Cardiff and have held visiting professorships or visiting fellowships at the universities of Oxford, Bristol, Keele, Oxford Brookes and East London. I have won a number of awards, including a United Nations Global 500 award, presented to me by Nelson Mandela.

I have known Hector as a friend for over ten years and have followed his activities closely. I have come to see him as a man of integrity, who is prepared to make great sacrifices for the causes in which he believes. He is deeply committed to the protection of the natural world, and has dedicated much of his adult life to this end. He recognises that we are living through an extraordinary time, in which the planetary systems which give us life and which fill our lives with wonder and delight are gravely threatened by the unintended impacts of industrial technologies. He is aware of the remarkable speed with which these impacts are damaging the biosphere, and the inability or unwillingness of governments and regulators to contain them.

As the failure of the Earth Summit in June 2012 to produce anything other than platitudes shows, governments are not prepared to implement any of the measures required to protect the living planet from the impacts of industrialism, however damaging these might be. In seeking to act where governments will not, Hector is ahead of his time. Our descendents will look back on this period and ask what we were thinking, as we stood by and watched the destruction of the biosphere.

Hector is a man of great compassion and empathy. He has helped many people who are far poorer and less fortunate than himself, offering them shelter and many kindnesses. In some ways he is too kind, and has sometimes been exploited by people he has sought to help. It is his overwhelming feelings of empathy and compassion, his inability to put other people's suffering out of his mind, that drive him to try to defend the living systems which give us life. In seeking to protect the environment and our food supplies, he has put his own freedom at risk. He is perhaps the most unselfish and self-sacrificing person I know.

I see his action at Rothamsted as being consistent with his principles and beliefs. While I have a slightly different view of the project he contested there, I believe that he acted with sincerity and seriousness of purpose, putting the interests of the living world and its people ahead of his own. He had nothing to gain in acting as he did and a great deal to lose. Whether or not you agree with his perception of the threat from the wheat trials there, he behaved unselfishly for the perceived benefit of both people and the planet.

He accepts that what he did was prohibited by the law. But he also knows that the law protects property at the expense of the world's living systems and the future of humanity, and that sometimes citizens have a duty which extends beyond the confines of the law, to act for the greater good. I think that history will judge men like Hector kindly, just as it judges kindly the unselfish law-breaking of the Suffragettes, the Chartists and the Tolpuddle Martyrs. Just as the people of earlier generations sacrificed their liberty for the cause of democracy, and felt they had a higher duty to do so, so the people of this generation have a higher duty to sacrifice their liberty for the protection of the living world. When our children and grandchildren press us, in the decades to come, to explain what we did to defend the biosphere, aware as we were of the threats it faced, Hector at least will be able to give them a answer.

I am happy for this document to be put before the court.

George Monbiot

Request to guarantee product safety

Dear Manager,

Please will you sign this letter guaranteeing your customers that their health will not be affected when using these products that contain glyphosate, and assure that you accept responsibility for any harm that may occur to your customers' health.

Bearing in mind that your company places the health and safety of its customers at the foremost of its policy, we ask you to guarantee that it is safe for us to use them upon purchase from your store.

Product	Producer company	Signature for safety guarantee
Garden Path	Bayer	
Patio & Drive Weedkiller	Bayer	
Path And Patio Weed Killer	Pestshield	
Weed Killer	Pestshield	
Path and Patio	Doff	
Glyphosate weedkiller by	Doff	
Roundup Total Weedkiller	Monsanto	
Roundup Concentrate Weedkiller	Monsanto	
Roundup Tree Stump	Monsanto	
Resolva Xtra Tough	Westland	
Resolva Weedkiller 24H	Westland	
Root Blast- Total Weedkiller (very strong)	Barclay Chemicals R&D Limited	
Weedol Pathclear		
Weedol Lawn		
Systemic Path & Patio Weedkiller,	TESCO	
Rootkiller	Wilko	

Please sign below, if you can assure me/us and the rest of your store's customers that these products are safe to use.

Name and signature store manager   Date:

Store and address:

Things, however, don't always quite go how we expect in life .
. . Three days before the 'OFF GRID' festival I was walking
down a side street in my local town when somebody walked past
me with a blue rubber glove and touched mv leg. 'Pervert' I
thought to myself. Now . . .whether it was that OR simply the
huge strain/pressure I was feeling for the August 24th action
we will never know. Many activist colleagues believe I was
'got at' (I did speak briefly on the phone because I really
had to which was probably a mistake). What I do know is that
for the next few months I was fighting for my life . . .

It was the last day of the 'Off Grid' Fest and the last act
(finale) and playing were my favourite festival band - Seize
the Day. Moments before they started I entered the packed
marquee when ███████████ (who with ███████████ are the top
anti GMO activists this country's ever seen) came towards me,
eyes popping out of his head, who told me about the breaking
news re-poor 'DeWayne Johnson'.

The wooziness had been getting worse but I just held out to
the end of the Seize the Day set to make the announcement that
there was now irrefutable evidence that DeWayne Johnson was
terminally ill as a direct result of using 'Roundup' (sold by
Monsanto and Bayer as 'safe' for gardeners, farmers, spraying
school yards etc). Theo Simon — lead singer of Seize the Day
said after my ' announcement' that that was the best ending to
a gig he's ever encountered in 25+ years of performing. Elated
in a victory I never expected to see, I walked outside into
the fresh clean air and collapsed in agony.

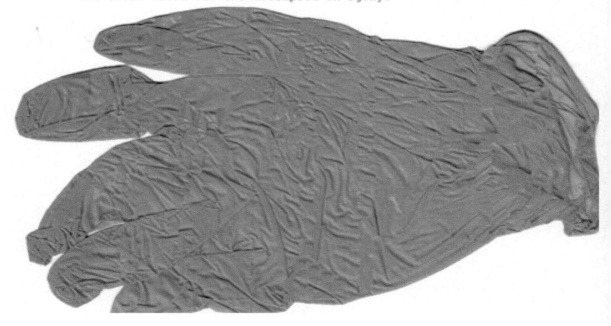

Martha

BAYER TO PULL GLYPHOSATE PRODUCTS, INCLUDING ROUNDUP, FROM U.S. HOME AND GARDEN MARKET.

Olivia Rosane. Jul.30,2021 02:00pm Est.

Roundup products on a shelf at a store in San Rafael on July 9th, 2018. Josh Edelstone/AFP via Getty Images.

Bayer will no longer sell glyphosate-containing products to US home gardeners, the company announced on Thursday.

The move comes as the company currently faces 30,000 legal claims from customers who believe use of these products cause cancer.

All very well BUT . . . .unless we ban the spraying of ALL Roundup – and any 'derivatives', the damage done by those huge booms overflowing with poison will do far more damage than a little spot spraying on unwanted 'visitors' in our back gardens. This is not to say we stop weeding - far from it – getting on our knees and doing 'something' every day is as honourable as anything.

Bayer's decision to end the U.S. residential sale of Roundup is a historic victory for public health and the environment. The "Center for Food Safety" executive director Andrew Kimbrell said in a statement . "As agricultural, large-scale use of this toxic pesticide continues, our farmworkers remain at risk. It's time for the EPA to act and ban glyphosate for all uses. . . .NOW.

The antithesis of eco-friendly lawn care. Glyphosate is a controversial ingredient because it has been linked to the development of non-Hodgkin lymphoma, as Cure noted. The World Health Organization's International Agency for Research on Cancer declared that it was "probably carcinogenic to humans," in 2015.

While the U.S. Environmental Protection Agency (EPA) under former President Donald Trump ruled that the chemical did not pose any risk to human health, the Biden Administration later admitted that the review was flawed and needed to be redone. It seems like President Biden understands these discrepancies – lets pray he doesn't go down the Obama pot hole.

JERUSALEM by Hector Christie

"And did those feet from ancient times

Walk upon England's mountains green

But now the cows burn in the pyres

This is the multinationals desire

And we've more supermarkets builded here

On England's once green and pleasant land"

Our 'piece de la resistance' had to be the Last Night of the Proms . . . . .I'd done a few other demos/marches with a group calling themselves 'Corporate Watch'. The group, largely made up with young, feisty women organised a meeting. I suggested we get thousands of the 'enclosed' sheets made up and give the fliers out at all the entrances stating the 'words for Jerusalem'.

It turned out EVERYBODY in the packed Albert Hall(too excited to have read the 'script')took the piece of paper and popped it into their pocket. Practically everyone in the Albert Hall got out their piece of paper (having read the all too familiar first lines before popping it back into their pockets — to be saved for the 'grand finale' no doubt . . . .).

The first two lines were boomed out with full gusto followed by nigh on silence as the coveted audience read about the horror of Foot and Mouth . . . . When the audience came to the 'third line' all suddenly went quiet — save for the 20 or so jubilant activists who'd cleverly 'mingled and dispersed' (motto for the day . . . .) covering all corners of the massive hall.

The indescribably horrendous murdering/killing of millions of farm animals in 2001 resulted in 100's of suicides. Many families came to see me after F&M to tell me their horrendous stories — of young farmers (and old) blowing their heads off when all their stock were annihilated. This when they had enough vaccines at around 99% efficiency to do all the cattle in the country — I have a document verifying this.

For more info on this and more check out 'The Final Curtain Call' plus I've written a 'spiritual' book — 'No Blade of Grass'

One of my proudest stories was at the last Oxford 'Real' Farming Conference I attended where I was introduced to David Murphy. David Murphy was, it transpired, Monsanto's et al Biggest most feared enemy. 'Monsanto/Bayer tried a number of ways to cleverly wipe him off the face of the planet – tampering with his brakes being just one example.

In conversation with David Murphy I mentioned (in front of my girlfriend) that it was I who climbed over the 14foot fence at Rothamsted and pulled Genetically Modified wheat – for which I had to report to the Police station every day for nearly 5 years. David Murphy exclaimed "My God was that you" to which I said 'yes' then David Murphy said . . . . "The news of that action went right across CNN news North America and it's solely down to 'you' that there's no commercial crops of GM wheat or GM barley being grown across the world".

I've always said that as activists, all we can do is 'delay, delay, delay using clever Direct Action/protest where needed to highlight what (you and I) might consider an important point. 'They' daren't have put me in prison because of the 'awareness' of what was going on behind the scenes was increasing by the day and people are now waking up faster than ever.

RIP THE CORPORATE WORLD NEVER TO RISE AGAIN

Countless demonstrations ensued going back to the early days of Foot and Mouth (see 'The Final Curtain Call – si vous interess'e). To give a few examples . . . .With a motley, but focussed – group, we'd infiltrate Corporate AGM's 'mingle and disperse' and see how many questions we could get. Our record was 6 out of 7 questions – the topic . . . . Genetic Modification. In a similar vein we'd pay regular visits to Nobel House, Smith Square; stand with Michael Meacher – the then Environment Minister outside Parliament soon before he died; We also did an 'Occupy' demo 10 miles outside Cambridge where I did a half hour talk with 90 or so 'employees' watching from on high flanked by 2 of the largest Neanderthal like monsters I've ever seen. We then erected the pop-up (very scruffy of course) 'Occupy' tents when we heard a fleet of sirens hurtling into the car park where we slipped round the back and made out way to 'Occupy' St. Pauls.

Where is Glyphosate Banned?
Updated August 2021

Numerous cities, counties, states and countries throughout the world have taken steps to either restrict or ban glyphosate, the active ingredient in Monsanto's Roundup weed killer.

The following countries have issued outright bans on glyphosate, imposed restrictions or have issued statements of intention to ban or restrict glyphosate-based herbicides, including Roundup, over health concerns and evidence uncovered in the Roundup cancer litigation proving the weed killer's link to cancer.

Argentina: In 2015, more than 30,000 health care professionals advocated for a glyphosate ban following the International Agency for Research on Cancer's (IARC) report on glyphosate, which concluded the chemical is probably carcinogenic to humans. More than 400 towns and cities in Argentina have passed measures restricting glyphosate use.

Australia: Numerous municipalities and school districts throughout the country are currently testing alternative herbicides in an effort to curtail or eliminate glyphosate use. Many use steam technology for weed control on streets and in other public places.

Following a series of massive jury verdicts in Roundup cancer lawsuits in the United States, the Australian state of Victoria launched its own review of glyphosate. Two councils in Sydney have either banned or are in the process of banning glyphosate use, and eight other councils are reviewing the chemical.

Austria: In June of 2019, Austria announced that it planned to ban glyphosate within the year. Leader of the Social Democrats, Pamela Rendi-Wagner, said she is "pleased" that her party's long-standing effort to ban glyphosate in Austria would "finally pay off" now that her party's motion had a majority in the Austrian parliament. The measure to ban glyphosate passed in July 2019. While the Austrian glyphosate ban was scheduled to take effect on Jan 1, 2020, the country's caretaker leader announced she would not sign the ban into law, citing a technicality. For now the ban is tabled.

Bahrain: According to Oman's Ministry of Agriculture, Bahrain and five other countries in the Gulf Cooperation Council (GCC) have banned glyphosate.

Barbados: The government announced that people will need a licence to purchase glyphosate. The new rule was designed to help manage the use of pesticides considered harmful to human health.

Belgium: Banned the individual use of glyphosate. In 2017, Belgium voted against re-licencing glyphosate in the EU. The country was also one of six EU member states to sign a letter to the EU Commission calling for "an exit plan for glyphosate . . ." The city of Brussels banned the use of glyphosate within it's territory as part of its "zero pesticides" policy.

Bermuda: Outlawed private and commercial sale of all glyphosate-based herbicides. In 2017, the government relaxed its ban on glyphosate, allowing the Department of Environment and Natural Resources to import restricted concentrations of glyphosate for managing roadside overgrowth.

Brazil: In August of 2018, a federal Judge in Brasilia ruled that new products containing glyphosate could not be registered in the country. Existing regulations concerning glyphosate were also suspended, pending a re-valuation of toxicological data by Anvisa, the country's health agency.

In September 2018, a Brazilian court overturned the federal judge's ruling. September marks Brazil's first month of soybean planting. The country is the largest exporter of soybean in the world and as such, has become heavily reliant on agrochemicals. Anvisa issued a statement following the courts decision to overturn the ruling, saying it will take necessary legal and technical steps in response.

Further, Brazil's Solicitor General's office has said it is preparing an appeal to the court decision with support from the Agricultural Ministry. Brazil's health agency concluded a re-valuation of glyphosate in February of 2019. Based on the Agency's findings, a blanket ban on glyphosate in Brazil is <u>unlikely.</u>

Canada: Eight of the ten provinces in Canada have some form of restriction on the use of non-essential cosmetic pesticides, including glyphosate. Vancouver has banned private and public us of glyphosate, <u>aside from the treatment of invasive weeds.</u> In June of 2019, New Brunswick officials announced that the province would reduce glyphosate spraying in certain areas with the promise that more regulation will follow.

Colombia: In 2015, Colombia outlawed the use of glyphosate to destroy illegal plantations of coca, the raw ingredient for cocaine, out of concern that glyphosate causes cancer. In March of 2019, President Ivan Duque asked for the judicial ban on aerial glyphosate spraying to be lifted. However, in July of 2019, the court maintained the judicial ban on glyphosate, ruling <u>that the government has to prove that glyphosate is not harmful to human health and the environment in order for the ban to be lifted.</u>

But Kenneth R. Feinberg, the Washington lawyer who oversawe the mediation process, said he expected most current claimants to eventually sign on to the settlement.

"In my experience, all those cases that have not yet been settled will quickly be resolved by settlement," said Mr. Feinberg, best known for running the federal September 11th Victim Compensation Fund. "I will be surprised if there are any future trials." . . .?

Bayer said the amount set aside to settle current litigation was $8.8 billion to $9.6 billion - Including a cushion to cover claims not yet resolved. It said the settlement included no admission of liability or wrongdoing - ie Next to nothing.

Individuals, depending on the strength of their cases will receive payments of $5,000 to $250,000, according to two people involved in the negotiations.

The coronavirus outbreak, which has closed courts across the country, may have pushed the plaintiffs and the company to come to any agreement.

"The pandemic worked to the advantage of settlement because the threat of a scheduled trial was unavailable," Mr. Feinberg said.

Talks began more than a year ago at the prompting of Judge Vince Chhabria of U.S.District court in San Francisco, who was overseeing thousands of federal courts and other jurisdictions.

The $1.25 billion set aside for future plaintiffs will be applied to a class-section suit being filed in Judge Chhabria's court on behalf of those who have used Roundup and may later have health concerns.

Part of the $1.25 billion will be used to establish an independent expert panel to resolve two critical questions about glyphosate: Does it cause cancer, and if so, what is the minimum dosage or - exposure level that is dangerous?

If the panel concludes that glyphosate is a carcinogen, Bayer will not be able to argue otherwise in future cases - and if the experts reach the opposite conclusion, the class action's lawyers will be similarly bound.

Pressure on Bayer for a settlement has been building over the past year after thousands of lawsuits piled up and investors grew more vocal about their discontent with the company's legal approach.

When Bayer, the giant chemical and pharmaceutical maker, acquired Monsanto two years ago there was a legal firestorm over claims that the herbicide, Roundup, caused cancer.

Now Bayer is moving to put those troubles behind it, agreeing to pay more than $10 billion to settle tens of thousands of claims while continuing to sell the product without adding warning labels about it's safety.?

The deal, announced Wednesday, is among the largest settlements ever in U.S. civil litigation. Negotiations were extraordinarily complex, producing separate agreements with 25 leading law firms whose clients will receive varying amounts.

"It's rare that we see a consensual settlement with that many zeros on it," said Nora Freeman Engstrom, a professor at Stanford University Law School.

Bayer, which inherited the litigation when it bought Monsanto for $63 billion, has repeatedly maintained that Roundup is safe.

Most of the early lawsuits were brought by homeowners and groundskeepers, although they account for only a tiny portion of Roundup's sales. Farmers are the biggest customers, and many agricultural associations contend glyphosate, the key ingredient in Roundup, is safe, effective and better than available alternatives.

The settlement covers an estimated 95,000 cases and includes $1.25 billion for potential future claims from Roundup customers who may develop the form of cancer known as non-Hodgkin's lymphoma.

The company is taking a calculated risk that the benchmark settlement will largely resolve it's legal problems. Bayer still faces at least 30,000 claims from plaintiffs who have not agreed to join the settlement.

Werner Bauman, Bayer's chief executive, said that the two critical conditions for a settlement were that it was financially reasonable and that it would bring closure to the litigation.

SHOCKING . . . . . .

"We are totally convinced" this does both, Mr. Baumann said in an interview on Wednesday. There is money put aside for existing claimants outside of the agreement, he said, and a structure to deal with future claimants that could emerge.

Fletch Trammell, a Houston-based lawyer who said he represented 5,000 claimants who declined to join, disagreed. "This is nothing like the closure they're trying to imply," he said. "It's like putting out part of a house fire."

Costa Rica: In December 2019, the country's National System of Conservation Areas issued a guideline prohibiting the use of glyphosate in Costa Rica's 11 Protected Wild Areas. The glyphosate restrictions also applies to the National System of Conservation Areas' institutions.

Czech Republic: Agriculture Minister Miroslav Gtoman said the country will limit glyphosate use starting in 2019. Specifically, the Czech Republic will ban glyphosate as a weed killer and drying agent.

Denmark: The Danish Working Environment Authority declared glyphosate to be carcinogenic and has recommended a change to less toxic chemicals. Aalborg, one of the largest cities kin Denmark, issued private use of glyphosate ban in September of 2017. In 2018, the Danish Governemt implemented new rules banning the use of glyphosate on all post-emergent crops to avoid residue on foods.

El.Salvador: In 2013, the country adopted a law banning glyphosate over links to deadly kidney disease. However, by 2016, the legislation appeared to stall.

Fiji: The government announced in March 2020 that glyphosate will be banned in the country effective January 2021 – Q – Done it yet?

France: French authorities banned the sale, distribution and use of Roundup 360 in early 2019. In May 2019, French Agriculture Minister Didier Guillaume announced that France would eliminate the use of glyphosate by 2021 with limited exceptions.?

Some 20 mayors throughout the country have banned glyphosate in their municipalities.

President Macron announced in December 2020 that the Government would offer financial aid to farmers who agreed to stop using glyphosate. The French President said in an interview with the media that while he still supports banning glyphosate he recognises that such products will be withdrawn from the market and no longer be permitted for use by the end of 2020.

Germany: Germany's cabinet passed legislation in February 2021 to ban glyphosate by 2024. German farmers will need to reduce the use of glyphosate until the ban takes effect in 2024. Certain retail stores in Germany have already pulled glyphosate-based herbicides like Roundup from shelves.

Greece: Greece was one of nine Eu countries to vote against re-licensing glyphosate in November 2017. The country was one of six EU member states to sign a 2018 letter to the European Commission calling for "an exit plan for glyphosagte . . ." According to Greek Minister of Agriculture Development Edvangelos Apostolou, " (i)t is our duty to push in the direction of risk management, in the interests of consumers, producers and the licence of Monsanto's Roundup against the wishes of Greek environmentalists.

India: In October of 2018, the government of Punjab banned the sale of glyphosate in the state. " All pesticides, manufacturers, marketers and dealers in the State shall not sell glyphosate formulations-concentrations with immediate effect. The licencing authorities have been asked to take the necessary steps for removal of entries of glyphosate from the licenses of 2019, issued by them," said the State Agricultural Secretary K.S.Pannu. In February 2019, the Indian state of Kerala issued a ban on the sale, distribution and use of glyphosate.

Italy: Italy's Ministry of Health placed a number of restrictions on glyphosate use. Italian legislators have also raised concerns about glyphosate safety, and have come out against re-licencing the herbicide in the European Union. In 2016, the Italian government banned the use of glyphosate as a pre-harvest treatment and placed restrictions on glyphosate use in areas frequented by the public. In November of 2017, Italy wa,

Luxembourg: The country will become the first in the EU to completely ban all products containing glyphosate. The Luxembourg glyphosate ban will take effect in three phases. On Feb 1st, 2020, market authorization was withdrawn. Stocks of glyphosate may be used until June 30th, 2020. On Dec 31st, 2020, the total ban on glyphosate will take effect.

Malawi: In April 2019, Malawi's Principle Secretary of the Ministry of Agriculture, Irrigation and Water development told the countries National newspaper that import licences for glyphosate-based herbicides like Monsanto's Roundup will be suspended immediately.

Malta: In July of 2019, Malta banned the use of glyphosate in public spaces. The spraying of glyphosate will not be allowed on roadsides or near schools, among other places.

The list is endless — plus it's all on the Internet should you wish to know more.

With thanks from Hector.

2001 Hand, Foot and Mouth Anti-Cull
Demonstration - S.Devon

GM Demonstration

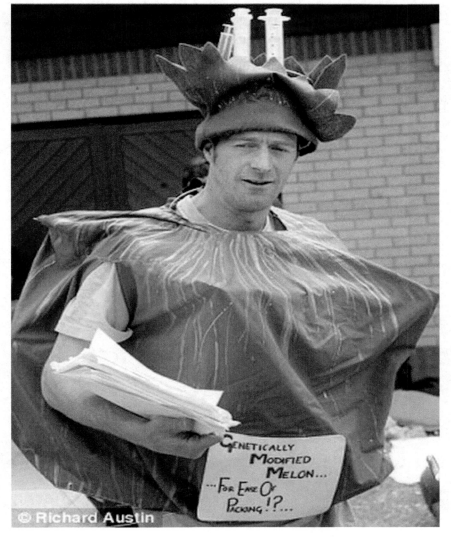

Hartland

24.5.2018

Agri Activism presents the

Roundup the Roundup — The 'warmup'

'4 Supermarkets and a Garden Centre Demonstration'

Yesterday a group of 8 of us set off for a first of a series of demonstrations against Monsanto's favourite herbicide — ROUNDUP.

We started at the 'Value House' near Atlantic Village where 3 of us (one carrying a camera phone) went down the aisles and filled our trolleys up with the highly toxic tubs of Glyphosate and its numerous derivatives — Resolve Extra tough root balls — Total weed killer (very strong) and Monsanto's Weedol, Pathclear and many more ALL with the same similar toxicity of Roundup/Glyphosate. To help give it more of an 'edge' 2 of us then wrapped the trolleys in our yellow and black tape saying . . ."

. . . .and all this in front of or near to the Managers who at the Value House were clearly irritated and listened a bit to us before issuing a few veiled threats and off we went

It was then to good old Walmart (sorry . .   .ASDA). As before 2 of us busied ourselves with quickly filling up our trolleys and just as we were wrapping our tape around the trolleys (which made a satisfyingly loud noise attracting the attention of a lot of shoppers) 'security' and 'Management' descended on us. They wanted to take our cameras and created a right furore - all of which was (secretly) filmed by a good friend of mine and seasoned Activist from the days of Globalise Resistance.

The 'threat' that sticks out the most - and there were a few, was when they told us that they would 'prosecute any of us who put this out on social media . . .' It was then off to a massive Tesco 'East the Water' where we geared up for more 'hostility'. But we couldn't have been more WRONG.

After the battering we had at ASDA, leaving us a little on edge, we entered Tesco. Here we filled up the trolleys but we ended up a bit confused when no one batted any eyelid. We went to customer service who were nothing but utterly charming.

JOY

4 Supermarkets and a Garden Centre

PART 2   30.5.18   4PM

Numbers escalated to the max - 14 people inclusive of 'seasoned' activists from the days of Global Resistance, Climate Camp (Heathrow), Reclaim the Streets, War on Want, 'Occupy'- to name but a few.

After the hostile reception we got at the Bideford ASDA the week before we were on full alert when we, in 3 cars, approached the (larger) ASDA in Barnstaple. One member of this elite posse had taken me aside earlier and explained my chaining myself to a metal upside down U frame would be pointless and a bit 'weak'. He said if I were to do a proper job I'd need to chain myself to the doors of ASDA stopping customers from getting in or out - for which I'd "certainly get arrested". With double the dose of adrenaline flowing through my endocrine system (still fairly untainted by Roundup I feel due to the healthy food I'm privileged to have from our garden plus high quality meat from our purely grass fed Highland cattle) I agreed and mentally began building my energies to prepare for (what I felt to be the 'inevitable').

On arrival at ASDA a journalist was waiting and I did an interview after which we hit the forecourt, whipped out banners - one saying 'Sygenta, Monsanto we don't want your GMO's' and another (first used at the Hague 2 years ago which got us into a lot of trouble) saying "GMO's UK . . . .YOU GROW IT - WE'LL BURN IT" (a threat we don't make lightly)

I then approached the doors of ASDA with the heavy duty chains in my rucksack when . . . .Horror of Horrors - Automatic doors with NO handles or bars to chain myself to. (last time I looked they definitely had handles) 'should have done a proper rekkey myself' some b . . . . . .stormed into the supermarket and whispered in my ear.

The main body got straight into their stride and filled up their trolleys with Roundup from the shelves. When Tony, myself and a couple of others went in the group had filled up their trolleys and covered them (and some of the aisles) with the magic yellow and black tape (a sign of danger in the wild) saying . . ."Glyphosate Precautions . . .Causes Cancer (skull and crossbones) KEEP OUT".

The security had clearly been briefed NOT to behave with aggression and threats as per last week and hit the charm offensive "we understand where you're coming from bla bla" and, I'm ashamed to say, I'm a sucker for politeness so we packed up and off we went to our final destination where we'd complete our '4 Supermarkets and a Garden Centre' remit.

Sainsbury's were clearly fully primed and quite simply allowed us to do whatever we wanted . . .so, to make it 'slightly' interesting, we got, ███ ███████ – our folk musician in residence to get out his guitar. I then chained myself to some railings lying on the ground with banners scattered hither and thither where ████ blasted out the Tapeley (and GR) anthem "Our World is not for Sale" followed by a brilliant off the cuff nursery rhyme sing along about Sainsbury's . . .

"Don't buy Roundup weed killer
It will kill you dead
If you're shopping at Sainsbury's
Buy something else instead . . ."

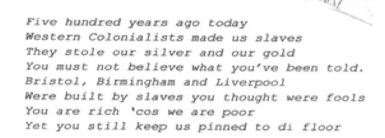

WHO OWES WHO?

Five hundred years ago today
Western Colonialists made us slaves
They stole our silver and our gold
You must not believe what you've been told.
Bristol, Birmingham and Liverpool
Were built by slaves you thought were fools
You are rich 'cos we are poor
Yet you still keep us pinned to di floor

Chorus a la Blair IP'S . . . .
'People killing people
People dying, multinationals always lying
They don't practice what they preach
They just turn the other cheek
Father Father Father help us
Give us guidance from above
Won't you tell me tell me tell me
Where is the love'

Chorus

A message to all in Africa
I'm Monsanto's boss Mr Shapira
We have some crops for you to plant
Do what you're told you'll get a grant
You may go hungry and be ill at night
Give us your land, don't try and fight
Cruel to be kind is the way I'll bet
To help you reduce your Third World debt

Chorus

Exploitation and Third World debt
Milk us all for what you can get
You are rich 'cos we are poor
Drop the debt get out the door.
Just one percent of interest
For our golf, diamonds and the rest
And you'd owe us 1,000 times more
Then we'd be rich and you'd be poor
Yes we'd be rich and you'd, be poor

Chorus

We corporate folk are here to assist
Turn your shabby hands into realms of bliss,
There'll be no more wars and no more sorrow,
Provided you give us your oil tomorrow,
We give you dams and GM crops
Our charity knows not where to stop
Homogenisation of our cultures
Will stop you all behaving like vultures
We're here to help, don't you get
It's good for you to pay your debt

Chorus

You control our foreign policy and take our land
To help pay a debt we don't understand
You dump your subsidised maize and cotton
Into a land the world's forgotten
This all in the name of globalisation
Which is tearing the heart out of our nation
Africans starving in their millions
As Corporate profits soar into trillions
You are rich 'cos we are poor
You have 'our' blood o your hands, that's for sure.

So who owes who? . . . . .Who owes who?
Who owes who? Why all the fuss? We don't owe you
YOU OWE US

- Contact local media – newspapers, radio, TV internet news e.g. Devon Live (or your equivalent). Tell them the date and location so they can attend/interview you.
- Make banners/posters/placards, visual impact is important. Yellow and black tape also provided to cover building/aisles-contact Hector for 'Activist Package'.

YELLOW+ BLACK TAPE

POSTER PAPER

PERMANENT MARKERS

COSTUME IDEA CARDS

SURVEY SHEET

- Make a costume (if you like) e.g. tomato, carrot, a bee or Vicar – anything to draw attention . . .
- 'Visit' Supermarkets/garden centres and fill baskets or trolleys with Roundup or other glyphosate based weed killer.
- Take goods to customer services or Management and ask **WHY** they are selling a known carcinogen, stress how you feel this should be banned as it harms children and wildlife.
- Present Manager/customer services with the sheet to sign and /or just information sheets.
- Stand outside with banners/placards do media interviews – PLEASE take photos or videos. Send to us.
- Even if you are on your own JUST DO IT!

WHY . . . . The New York Times October 29th 2016 . .
"An extensive examination by the NYT indicates Genetic
Modification in the US and Canada has NOT accelerated
increases in crop yields OR led to an overall reduction in the
use of chemical pesticides".

Dr. Steve Suppan writes on Trump Administration's Retreat from
Science-backed Regulations . . "Unfortunately, the commission
is not only retreating from its promise to regulate
nanotechnology . . .it is now cooperating with industry to
build a legal case for NOT risk assessing or regulating
products derived from new genetic engineering techniques . .
.".It's now open house in the US to tamper/alter food in any
way a scientist feels without risk of recriminations. Who
will be the next 'poodle' to embrace the latest fad from the
US?

11.5.2018

ROTHAMSTEAD . . . .PART 3

2 days ago on Sunday 6th May I paid Rothamstead Research Centre a visit on the way up to visit my Mum. I was just curious to see what they were doing in regard to trial plots — whether genetically modified or normal.

There's a number of ways into Harpenden — the nearest town, but as 'luck' would have it I suddenly got a glimpse of the 'Rugby car park' as I sped past (the spot I left my car in 6 years ago when I got into the trial plots). The rugby facilities had improved dramatically from my last visit which is why I nearly drove past.

The gate leading to the fences and trial plots instead of having strict 'Trespassers will be Prosecuted' etc warnings had a friendly banner advertising the local charity fair. I hopped over the gate and headed for the huge fences which had an extra fence around the GM etc crops from my first visit where there was just one large fence (— still doable I thought but might take a while longer). I'm not sure if they're still trialling GM crops (bet they are) and if not I'll send Huw Dylan Jones' successor a letter of thanks.

I should say at this juncture, I almost certainly wouldn't have gone to Rothamstead again were it not for Toby Bruce (the Manager of the trials on the ground) sending me the enclosed highly patronising e.mail — this when we'd been having a (what I felt) healthy line of conversation. Equipped solely with a camera phone I headed for the fence and, as in previous visits, felt completely safe and protected amongst the seemingly hundreds of (creepy) CCTV cameras. Armed with that sense of 'meant to be' I took pictures in my own time (still, I admit, expecting to be lifted/hear sirens at any moment) before heading back to the Rugby ground.

I was nearing Harpenden with 'larger' on my mind when 2 police cars full of cops hurtled past me at breakneck speed in the direction I'd just come from. I stress I didn't deliberately go up on a Sunday (seeing my dear Mum that evening was much more important). For me, personally, I'm probably getting a bit old for this kind of carry on but if we don't wake up to the HUGE dangers these horrendous multinationals pose to our very survival on earth we've had it. Imagine if Monsanto

(Bayer and the rest) came out tomorrow and apologised for Agent Orange and for forcing carcinogenic products on and into all corners of the globe with a declaration and promise to sort out the mess and suffering they've caused to land, watercourses, PEOPLE, nature and do all they can to clean up this stunning planet and feed the world healthy, chemical-free food? (see www.tapeleypark.com for info how we could nearly 'feed the world' twice over if 'we' had the volition/will).

TO WHOM IT MAY CONCERN

I have just received my annual box of RHS brochures in the usual big parcel containing leaflets which we have always displayed in our gift shop. I'm ashamed to say I've always been too wet/busy or both to make a stance against RHS policy of allowing/encouraging the use of Roundup in their gardens to control weeds. Lady Anne Palmer - a very close friend of may Mum when at Rosemoor, would be turning in her grave.

I have actively been campaigning against Roundup, Genetically Modified food and pesticides in general which I believe are killing millions of farmers, animals, ordinary people and children. It is currently sprayed in towns and school playgrounds and is absorbed through the feet of children who go barefoot - as it does into our pet's feet.

Any doubts about what I am saying have been eradicated since the black farm worker, Dewayne Johnson in California, was recently diagnosed with terminal cancer as a direct result of spraying Roundup. We at Tapeley stopped spraying chemicals a few years ago and yes it was hard at the start, with 'weeds' growing up in the paths and any gaps containing soil. I was out with others pulling the wretched things and ….. yes, 'cursing' the little blighters at times especially when those small green shoots erupted again just days later.

These days, however, there are more and more alternatives to carpet bombing chemicals. Flame guns are effective but not good for the environment of course. Zac Goldsmith has funded a kind of foam gun which works but again more expensive. It might sound 'odd' but we are now in our fifth year (of being chemical free) and you get used to keeping on top of the more important areas. Also, our Jenny - who is from the Physic garden in London before being lured in by Tapeley's now established Permaculture garden, has experimented with mixtures of cider vinegar, citronella and other 'ingredients' which have proven very adept at keeping most weeds at bay. If it works, we will patent it and name it 'Strictly Roots'.

MOST importantly is everybody has noticed the huge difference in biodiversity - of animals, insects, bird life etc and, as well as the traditional holiday makers, a lot more ecologically orientated visitors have been coming to Tapeley - this due to the huge escalation of wildlife since we banned Roundup 5 or so years ago. Woodpeckers, bats, insects, grass snakes, adders - which keep the pesky mice under control etc etc, are now thriving - you literally see them everywhere.

I've just found out that this situation is far more serious than I thought … In the news yesterday it was reported that all insect life in the world could be eradicated within 100 years. (It is reckoned 20% of insects could be wiped out in just 20 years). Insects are, of course, a vital part of our food chain and with farmers spraying more chemicals than ever we really are heading headlong for a doomsday scenario. Many people have noticed fewer insects in their gardens and when did you last see a few insects spattered over your windscreen whilst driving ? We all need to wake up and act.

Yesterday I visited RHS Rosemoor just outside the 'spectacular' town of Torrington. I wasn't expecting to find any Roundup being that it's winter and the weeds aren't really growing yet. As you can see from the photos, roundup is 'gaily' displayed on shelves in the Rosemoor shop. I really believe the RHS has a real duty to abandon the policy that every plant, shrub etc needs to look pristine throughout its lifespan. This especially in the light of recent evidence that ordinary folk who handle/use this product can contract cancer and potentially die.

I'm the 'caretaker' (I don't believe in 'ownership') of a 6000 acre estate in North Devon and, probably through guilt (ridiculous I know) given a home to anyone who wishes to live here if there's a space - which hasn't been easy I admit. Awareness of the dangers of pesticides is now very much acknowledged and we've recently found out - having put out to tender, that there are now more farmers than ever who wish to farm 'chemical free'. I sincerely believe that this is our chance to be a part of a really exciting change and there's nothing that would make me (and others) happier than if the RHS swing into action and embrace a future of chemical free, organic agriculture. I look forward to the thoughts of the Royal Horticultural Society.

Copies sent to all RHS outlets, The Historic Houses Association HHA), and other interested parties.

We look forward to your thoughts/ideas on this important matter.

With sincere best wishes

HECTOR CHRISTIE

STOP SPRAYING NOW - PLEASE

Dear Gerald, Liz and Joyti, (and 1or2 others-like Bidi, Bill and Jim, to keep them in the picture)

I have just come off the phone to Paul (from Bindmans) who had all the information Mike Schwartz has. I asked him if we could have a meeting? He asked the reason and I said to find out if we could have the High Court Injunctions dropped on Gerald, Liz and Joyti and myself(but said I'm not so bothered about me) and do these injunctions get dropped automatically after 3 years as we anticipate?

Paul said the only way the injunctions would get dropped is if we applied for a court hearing for them to be dropped. Paul made the point that the Judge would perceive/state that the only reason for making such an application would be so that we can go out and pull more crops and we'd be wheeled out of court with a biggish bill to pay and nothing gained. He said the injunction may or may not be due to my getting into the enclosure but, either way, the 'incitement' to do criminal damage and encourage others to do the same is enough to keep us all bound and if we do break the injunction much longer prison sentences/confiscation of property etc would be the result. He said he knows it worked before - but that was with a few smaller trial plots. He pointed out the whole point of clever activism is to keep changing the battle field (which we all, of course, 'inherently' know) and find clever ways to inform and win the public over onto our side on a grand scale.

When I put the phone down, I felt I'd received a bollocking/dressing down from my Headmaster. This in a way was confirmed when I found an e-mail sent to me by Mike Schwartz - the main man at Bindmans Solicitors who'd done so much for me over my lengthy court cases after pulling GM wheat plants (and scattering organic seed) at Rothampstead Research Centre on May 20th 2012. He wrote "thanks for the call/message earlier. Sorry I could not speak. I think your queiry is one better picked up by my colleague, Paul, to whom you spoke a while ago?"

It was like having a great mirror being held up in front of me. For the past 4 months or so since my dear Dad died, I've submerged (more than ever) into the anti-GM campaign especially since it looks more than likely the commercial growing of GM crops will be given

the green light next year due to the Trans Atlantic Trade Agreement
(TTIP) - indeed this has been the major topic discussed at Activist
oriented Festivals I've attended this summer.

Three months ago I had 20,000 cards titled 'Resistance is
fertile' (accompanied by the symbol of a scythe) printed and nigh
on 18,000 have gone out to people with my (and others') details
inviting people to "join others in pledging to fight against the
growing of GM crops in the UK." Because (I know) my e-mails are
intercepted I (and others) have asked everybody to respond to this
by post. We 'thoroughly' covered the Big Bristol Carnival (St.Pauls),
Glastonbury, the 'Globalise Resistance' Festival here at Tapeley
(who've circulated cards to groups in London and Brighton), The
Green Gathering and (most enthusiastic of all) a big trendy wedding
up here 2 weeks ago attended by all the big Festival organisers -
Rabbit hole etc.

I have not received one single response so I contacted some
people who've ALL said that they have sent me pledges with their
details. Devastated (and angry) I've realised that all my
(handwritten - bills still get through) mail has been 'intercepted.'
I still feel if 'they'd' been vaguely clever (which fortunately
they're not) they'd have let a few sheets through to make it seem
people really didn't give a s . . . anymore.

Over and above this I've organised small demonstrations in
towns, cities and villages across the country against GM and helped
with the March Against Monsanto in London. All this accompanied by
cards and thorough and varied information sheets (A4 sheets for those
wishing to know more and A5 smaller fliers who want the bullet
points). The more I find out about GM the worse it is - for human
health and the environment, and simply revolves around the control
of our food chain by a few purely profit-driven huge multinationals
- there is now more money going into Agriculture (GM) than Fracking,
nuclear/anything.

My dear and beloved friend, Daphne, who has done more for me
than anyone and is my right arm (holding me together) said to me
(before my recent little holiday to Wales to see Gerald) that I was
in danger of making myself ill. Since my Rothampstead exploits - 3
stressful court cases, warnings from activist friends my 'life was
in danger,' endless threatening letters re. confiscating belongings
(hence no car in my name, bank a/c etc), visits from bailiffs and
likelihood of prison (where I vowed to go on hunger strike until we
had a proper/fair debate - I even 'prepared' by not eating for a few
days) etc, it's been a bit full on at times.

We must have ruffled them a little bit, because in a recent
article in the Telegraph (5.8.14) about GM flax with 'vital' extra
Omega-3 (why not just plant lots of hemp . . .?) they go on about
. . ."unlike previous trials, where protesters scaled the fence and

organised demonstrations outside Rothampstead, the trial has proceeded without problems . . .it does sort of look like Guantanamo . . .I think consumers find it easier to swallow when they know you are engineering a plant for health benefits rather than to repel insects (as per GM wheat -now, I believe, 'pulled' - excuse the pun)."

In addition to this I'll come clean about putting every penny I've been able to get my hands on has gone into the cause which has less than impressed the powers that be in my life (my dear Dad would have disowned me if he had known). Most of the money went to the 'Occupy' movement and GM. There's very little left and I don't wish for that money to be used for fighting what I call 'rearguard battles.' As mentioned earlier, I'd like these funds to be used wisely for a campaign to inform/win public support, by organising meetings with Ministers, local Councillors/sustainability groups, the WI (vital), whole food groups, land owners, anti 'Fracking Groups- we must, I feel, work together for more sustainable energy and safe/healthy food AND . . .setting up GM free regions. In the same vein, I believe the 'pledge' needs to be cleverly worded, sensitive and inspiring. The general public are totally turned off to all things radical I feel after what's going on in the Middle East - horrific beheadings etc and the Ukraine.

Funnily enough, this whole peaceful/gentler approach came to me in a flash as I was driving myself to play football this afternoon when in an instant everything lifted and (windows down in Appledore) I found myself belting out . . "I can see clearly now the rain has gone . ." and as I sang the word 'gone' . . .that song came on the radio and (singing along) I felt the biggest weight I've ever had lifting off my shoulders and blazed in with a hat-trick.

In the same vein I know this all ties in perfectly with my Dad . . . The last 2 nights I've (for the first time since he died) had consecutive dreams about my Dad. The first was about him being on his own - seemingly in a gloomy, quiet but peaceful 'contemplative' place, where he surprised me by getting up to go to the toilet. Then last night I was by his bed with Mum. He was looking chipper, bathed in light and smiling (he had the most wonderful smile I've ever seen). He asked us if he could take us out to lunch which we did where he sumptuously sipped his way through some of his favourite red wine. It was as if his 'contemplative' phase was over and he was off to the light. This morning I rang Mum and got his (her) housekeeper. I asked Patricia how Mum was and she said she was in France with friends and was feeling relaxed and happy for the first time. I 100% believe in the spirit world (written a book about it after all) and to me it was a sign to change direction. All suggestions welcome . . . .

Thank you for taking the time to read this.
Hector
Ps Please could you ring or e-mail me as soon as you receive this

so I know you've received it.

PPs I wonder if anyone could e-mail me more details about Roundup which I believe is such a good massive door opening subject. As I understand it (lost bits of paper) it's the Glyphosate on it's own that's been tested without the so called adjuvants (toxic chemicals which break down the plant cell walls without which the Glyphosate wouldn't work). I'm not totally clear on this, so any help would be gratefully received. ALSO (and equally importantly) . . . .does anyone of you know of the most effective eco-friendly (and cost effective) weed killer we could recommend to farmers? I've always felt it hard to be 'anti' something unless you are pro a positive alternative - financially similar and effective. Salt we've found to be particularly effective but some say 'it kills worms and microorganisms but it's cheap. There's also a guy called Richard Jackson who advertises a double action weedkiller he calls 'Flower Power'. We at Tapeley have been 'experimenting' with mixtures of cider vinegar, soap suds, salt etc; plus flame throwers and boiling water (and pulling the buggers by hand). They're all a bit hit and miss and tend to work much better on hot, dry days. (If we come up with a cost effective mix that works we will let you know and any ideas you might have please let us know.) Thank you.

Rothamstead Research centre de-brief

A wee 'Action' de-brief on Rothamstead Research Centre on ….
(Ps. Sara's detailed account of what was said to come . . .the
'juicy bit' of what was said)

Since I entered Rothamstead Research Centre on 24.5.2012
where I pulled GM wheat plants and scattered organic wheat, I
have been 'monitored' very closely. Not only are e-mails opened
(as many peoples' are) but my mail too - the evidence surfaced
last year and the year before when I and my girlfriend gave out
1000's of info sheets and 'cards' for people to sign up to pull
GM crops when they're grown in the UK (or just say they don't
want them). 100's of people said they responded but not one was
allowed through (if 'they'd' have had half a brain they'd have
allowed some through and I'd have thought . . . "oh well people
aren't bothered . . .").

One of the other consequences of Rothamstead and all
those wretched court cases when all 'they' did was try to shut
me up and mess up my head in any way possible, was they 'banned'
me from Hertfordshire. Just as I abided by my bail conditions -
reporting to Barnstaple police station every day for ages, I
stayed out of Hertfordshire. This was a shame for me as I have
good friends in this county. Breaking bail is an imprisonable
offence and with a relatively clear diary for the first time
ever felt this was the time to test it. Doubling it up by vowing
to go on Hunger Strike should I be 'banged' up (until such time
we force scientists from 'both' sides to come together and agree
on a methodology and work together in the name of humanity to
find out whether feeding ourselves, our children and dogs GM
food/roundup ready crops is 'safe' . .or not . . .)and off Sara
and I went.

The uncertainty of not knowing when you might get pulled
over and (with my track record}the idea of wrapping the Snow
White Monsanto posters round the Rothamstead Research Centre
with yellow tape warning . . .   "NO ENTRY -Disease Control
Precautions" . . . .and I felt there was a high likelihood I'd
be carted off.

Sara and I bedded down the night before with the 'usual'
restless night and set off after breakfast. My heart definitely
sped up as we entered Harpendon where we rather nervously drove
back and forth past the Rothamstead Research Centre when we
settled on the best option . . . to go to the Pub. Here I
ordered 2 'spicy' tomato juices and put my foot down when Sara
demanded a whiskey.

'Clueless' we then drove to the Research Centre again
before agreeing to leave the car at the Pub where we stocked up
with posters etc and set off on the 15 or so minute walk to the
'Centre'. On getting there I stood in front of signs saying . .
'Rothamstead Research Centre' and BBSRC (- Biotech Industry).

Here Sara took photos of me holding a poster composed by my good friend/artist, who has done loads for me, called Mark 'Dreddy' (for obvious reasons when you meet him) Brassington (he, to me, makes Banksey seem like an amateur).[The picture depicts a beautiful (but dead) Snow White under a pile of bright red apples with a Monsanto banner plugged in at the top, and the poisonous apple, from which she'd recently taken a bite, having rolled away with caption . . "poisoning us since 1901" – when Monsanto was 'formed', having rolled out of her hand. The (simple) message alongside reads as follows: " We demand long-term INDEPENDENT testing to prove GM food is safe for us to eat/feed our children and safe for the environment – i.e. It will not cross-pollinate with conventional or organic crops." What was interesting was following our little 'caper' I showed the poster to Toby Bruce, who I felt was a genuinely nice guy, who said that that was what they did at Rothamstead. Maybe this is something I could follow up on?]. Then on looking through windows we saw plaster falling off the walls and the whole place (riddled with CCTV cameras on the outside – probably not working) looking unloved and unoccupied. We then walked to the end of the building and saw all manner of plush lunar module style buildings and lots of people walking speedily to a building on our left oh . .and lots of 'modern'CCTV cameras.

At this point I approached a lady and gentleman and said "Excuse me, can you tell me where I can find Huw Dylan Jones (his was the only name I knew and was the Chief Scientist at Rothamstead when I 'got in' where he told a wee 'porky' saying I pulled 550 plants when I pulled 3 and lots of leaves, and scattered organic wheat seed etc etc)." To this the lady asked "if I was here for the seminar . . . .?" This momentarily scrambled my head, but having been in such situations a few times (e.g. Labour Party conference 2004, G8 Edinburgh 2005) I said "Yes and I'm very much looking forward to it" to which the lady said . . "yes there's a lot of interest from scientists being it's 'his' last presentation before retiring to Aberystwyth . . . ." " yes, he'll be much missed" I said – an excited glow forming in my heart. "Do you have a pass?" the lady asked to which I said "no". She then said "quick . . .you won't have time to fill out all the forms (presumably of the department I worked in, my subject etc etc) so just write your names". This we did and an official pass was placed over our heads and we were hurried into the Conference – the last to arrive before Huw started.

As I walked to a seat, I was blown away by what was happening (I nearly went to the front directly facing Huw but knew this was cruel so chose seats near the back). Sara noticed Huw's face as we entered and said his jaw dropped through the floor and he looked like he'd seen a ghost. (I deliberately 'politely' refrained from catching his eye).

Poor Huw (I genuinely did feel sorry for him) began his 'parting speech' with a prolonged stutter. I'd seen Huw doing talks before on the net where he was slick and articulate. The stutter played a good 30-40% role in his talk. He was presumably wondering a how on earth did I 'get in' and when was I going to leap up to vociferously 'lend' my opinion to the proceedings a la heckling Tony Blair and Gordon Brown, or (worse still . . .) when would I get up and pull my trousers down as I did on Breakfast TV in 2005 which sent Natasha Kaplinsky and Adrian Charles into a spin.

No sooner than we sat down than the lady and gentleman who'd quickly ushered us in (who 'coincidentally' were the ones who were organising the event – hence the fastracking of our entrance) came and sat behind us. During Huw's presentation, when Sara and I were behaving very normally (not easy for me obviously) – taking notes and listening with a high degree of interest (albeit with not a clue as to what he was talking about in my case – not Sara's . . .), there was endless movement across the room with folk whispering messages into different people's ears. To this I sincerely thought 'how disruptive this carry on must be for poor Huw – and this in his farewell speech, no wonder his stutter was getting worse'.

When he'd finished, it was time for questions. My hand was first to go up needless to say, but a gentleman the other side of the room was chosen before me. I caught the guy with the mike's eye and he nodded as if to say 'I'd be next'. However, by then the shuffling (and whispering) around the room had escalated even more.

Just as I was beginning to lose faith with the guy with the mike who was clearly avoiding me (by then it was clear to a reasonable minority I was, indeed, an imposter), Huw indicated to the mike man that I speak. I began by saying "How honoured I was to be here at Huw's farewell talk . . .However, Huw, early on you mentioned the use of 'Surfactants' just once and as I understand it Monsanto's Glyphosate/Roundup wouldn't work without these additives/adjuvants which break down the strong cellular plant walls which then allows the Glyphosate to kill the weed – the GM crop being 'modified' to be resistant to the highly toxic Roundup – which then goes straight into our food chain of course . . .. From what I can gather, the GERMAN'S BFR (our equivalent of DEFRA) responsible for the safety of our food/chemicals used currently, use less than 90 different surfactants (many are simply animal fat/inert substances) due to thwe health risks associated with how different chemicals 'react' together. However, in this country with over 400 different surfactants added to glyphosate with seemingly little

162

or no safety checks in place, and it seems those with influence don't really care about the health implications to the public . . .?"

At this moment Huw cut me short stating "we are not really here to discuss safety issues or GM . . . .(even though his whole talk had been about inserting all manner of genes into other cells to create this, that, or the other supposedly beneficial traits) . . However, Hector, maybe it's time you introduced yourself to those in this room . . .?" I stood up then stated that . . "It was me that some 3½ years ago scaled the fence at your Research Centre where I pulled plants and scattered organic wheat seed . . ." The room erupted in a wave of gasps, a clasping of cheeks, and leaping up from their seats. It was explained afterwards that this, being Huw's last speech, was strictly invite only for long serving 'trusted' scientists from all over the place – such was the delicacy of the 'science' under discussion.

Following this, the seminar was pretty much wrapped up immediately and Sara and I were invited for coffee and nibbles by the Head honchos including Huw, Toby Bruce, a (very bright) Greek lady and others all of whom were kindly very eager to speak with us.

They tried to reassure us that any crops trialled met with rigorous safety checks- whether GM or otherwise (which I admitted to not being quite convinced about – who were the 'independent' assessors I asked?). I said that we have scientists/very practical knowledgeable people on our side of the fence who would love to work with Rothamstead scientists. Toby Bruce, a good man I feel, was at pains to reassure me GM trials were far from the major emphasis of Rothamstead. I said that I knew and accepted that was true (I forgot to ask about the GM flax trialled after the GM wheat failure – damn). I reiterated my HUGE concern at the time that wheat was a grass species which (as I understood it) meant wheat pollen with a cow gene in it (as was the case – this to 'possibly' repel aphids) could mean 'when' the GM wheat flowered and released pollen into the air it could alter the genetic code of the world's most prolific vegetation – grass. This, I said, "is why the Angels helped me fly over your fence . . ."

Some wince when we activists speak of Angels, but, like others before an action I always offer myself up saying to the 'Angels' (I have so much proof of angellic help – not just protecting me in the phenomenal riots in Genoa 2001, Climate Camp Heathrow etc etc but day to day 'miracles' which we ALL of us get the same – it's just most of us chose-normally because of fear, not to listen) . . . "Let thy will be done." . . .as we always say. Indeed my girlfriend will vouch I said this over and over as we approached Harpendon – and this just for sticking a few posters on a wall . . . I wrote a book in the mid 90's embracing all the religions about this and, like we ALL do should we choose to listen, have had 1000's of examples of miraculous proof.

My book is called called 'No Blade of Grass . .' (is blown without divine intervention) - i.e. everything happens for a reason and the timing is perfect if we go with the flow and 'Trust'. In my time as an activist, trying simply to do my miniscule part in helping safeguard a world fit for my children and theirs - with no volition for personal 'gain' for me (vital or it won't work), I've had endless examples. You only have to look at the perfect time of arrival at Rothamstead - the pffaffing around, Pub etc, meaning we arrived at the precise second meeting the organisers who whisked us in.

Another example is the Labour Party conference 2004 in Brighton where I was the first person to heckle the Prime Minister at his annual 'flagship' speech. It was George Monbiot's idea but I had a niggly feeling I'd be the only one to 'get in' - this when loads of us signed up 3 weeks before the event. There was coincidence after coincidence (another story) but a favourite 'inspirational' historical story for me was when Drake patiently finished his game of bowls, which took an hour when the Spanish Armada were closing in on our shores - much to the panic of his officers. On finishing the British fleet set sail and the tide changed at the perfect second where British guns were lined up to blow the Spanish away - else we'd be speaking Spanish now.

The conference opened on Sunday. My inclination was to leave Devon immediately BUT I wanted to play a game of football which I felt could jeopardise my chances, but all the same chose to play - a la Drake and his bowls. I drove up and on getting to the entrance (highly fortified as that year Al Qaeda were threatening to blow up the Brighton Centre) was refused entry and sent to Interpol round the corner. I was there for an hour thinking 'Oh well . . . .'when a huge policeman gave me my accreditation. "I must have filled out the form wrong" I said limply (but excitedly) . . "no the mistake was our end" he said . I coasted into the main hall where John Prescott was speaking and my heart sank. However, literally within 30 seconds Prescott wrapped up and the 'compere' announced . . 'the reason so many of you are probably here is to get a pass to see Blair speak on Tuesday . . .there are only enough tickets for half the delegates so it's first come first served'. I was fifth in the line for my accreditation. After speaking my mind 'at' the hapless (but loathsome) Blair I was 'roughed up' and taken to Brighton prison. Here the senior warden on duty poured over the internet etc for an hour - I gave him every bit of information about me, when he said . . "it's extraordinary there is absolutely no information about you anywhere". I sincerely believe the Angels/whatever do pull strings should we make ourselves 'available' and we are operating in accordance with Divine Will.

8 months later the same happened at the G8 Scotland when a Guardian journalist gave me a phone number to see if I could get into Brown's speech at the old Scottish Parliament. I spoke on my phone to a lady who said there were 2 tickets left . . "Goodie", I said "can I have one" . . .I gave her all my details and when I gaily went up to the desk and joyously introduced myself I was the only one not to get asked for ID and a 'media' card (it was only for journalists and I was 3 rows back from where Brown was due to speak.)

The wheat trial at Rothamstead was the same. I had no idea where it was or how I'd 'get in'. To cut to the quick the poor security guard on the CCTV left his camera tower to go to the toilet at 'precisely' the time I came out from the cover of the wood – I was keeping a record of the time. 'Rana Farood' obviously had problems 'downstairs' as I spent ages getting bits of wood from a forest (visualising an 'invisible' cloak as I walked within 100 yards of 3 security guards actually 'looking' my way, 4 times) to help me scale the fence.

The recent events at Rothamstead come under precisely the same umbrella. MOST importantly I believe in all of this is my (and other wonderful activists who do so much more than me to try to make the world a better place) actions would never have gotten off the ground without 'unseen' assistance. In precisely the same vein I believe VERY strongly that if we were not in alignment with the wishes of the angellic cosmic beings that are gently helping this world to wake up, respect and love the stunningly ravishing world we are so blessed to inhabit at this moment in time, we so called Activists (I say good people who lovingly care) wouldn't get out of the blocks with the ludicrous surveillance and paranoia dominating so many people's lives.

As I'm finishing off this piece the Ziggy Marley song . . "Tomorrow People where is your past . . ." is playing on the radio. Please let's work together for the betterment of mankind. I like so many, have many ideas – the crazy waste of 40% of our food due to shape and size being one example. We need a whole new approach to agriculture – most of us forget small farmers provide the world with 70% of it's food . . .

LET THY WILL BE DONE

Hector Christie

I am passing on copies of the 'Research' papers on what is being worked on currently – the 'Push-Pull' technology(Trap Crop) being trialled in Kenya looks particularly interesting, to some of our members which I hope is ok and which I hope will initiate dialogue.

The Christie Clan!

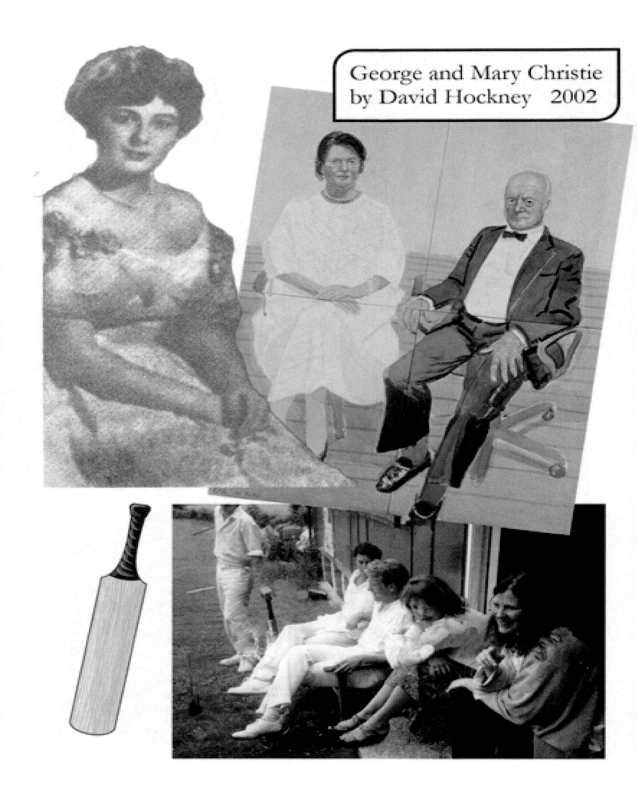

George and Mary Christie
by David Hockney   2002

Spiritual Reading by Harry Sida

Question: What is this 'knight' aspect I keep seeing time afer time after time in Hector?

Card: King of Air – Dost thou not remember me Hector? We have met many times before. Maybe you remember, maybe you remember me not. But thou remembers me. My convert name is Truth – Speaker, and I cannot deceive in any way yet the truth I speak can be twisted in your dense sphere. Trouble yourself not with the struggles that belong to others; it only wearies your heart and turns inward your attention. Let the quarrels of others be, it's no real concern of your true self who needs open spaces and the wind in your tousled hair! Oh how your thoughts skip and skip! How your emotions rise and fall! I see the dissatisfaction in your heart; know that I weep for thee. But know also how strong you shall become when you accept who thou art! I hold two swords with me; one is mine and rests in its scabbard at my side. The other is yours and I hold this in my hands. The scabbard and hilt are of gold, silver and copper, studded here and there with topaz, sunstone and citrines. But the blade, oh the blade! – is the purest, mirror bright steel, hard yet flexible and so sharp! This, my friend is a great sword of Truth and Justice! With its aid you can actively take part in the cleansing of your world through subtle means such as speech, actions and thought and feeling. Your word, when you grasp this sound, shall be the word of Truth. Your thoughts shall be as the deep blade, piercing through all deception, all illusion and all lies. Your eyes shall mirror back the falseness and illusion that you truly perceive, o the horror and terror of those who look you in the face with deception. Your deeds will be an example to men, for in your actions they shall see the light of the divine in action. It is a grave responsibility to take up tis sword, and vow that you can refuse if you so wish. You will not incur wrath and no guilt with besiege you. For this must be considered carefully by you, because once you pick up this sword, there is no turning back. If you do refuse, then I shall happily keep the sword for you, for it belongs to no other, until the time when you pass from your world to my kingdom. Here I shall pass it on to you with all the ceremony and honour, for you will, without doubt accept it then when the coarseness of your physical body is left behind but if you accept the sword whilst in incarnation, then the healing of Truth and Justice springs forth from your being and floods over wherever you go. This is the true knight, the knight that fights for the summerlands, the logres, that place of perfect peace profound. You will find that you will be liked and disliked, some may even hate you, but others will love you and will follow you. You may also suffer and be brought low in your world, but you shall never be without support and guidance and strength in times of need. If you would take up the sword, you only have to ask the Grey One (me) for my name and instruction on how to summon me. Then, when you have made a successful summoning of my peace and essence, the power of the sword I hold for you will be awakened. All you have to do then is to foster its growth and allow it to lead you. You have the freedom also to call me at any time for I would be most honoured to work with you and for you. The forces that I rule in my kingdom will be called upon again and again in the future to help your earth and all upon it to undergo the dying process and birthing process. During this transference process, the people shall call for the knights to protect them and to give them courage and will.

You will, upon reading this, doubt much and you may even feel that you cannot see yourself as this 'knight' Yet I would ask you to review some of Karen's channelling for you, also of Mickey's, there you will find, nestled amongst many truths, the choices that lead and point to what has been, written here. Fare you well young knight-to-be, maybe you will remember me soon!!

Question: I thank you, King of Air, for being the carrier of your name if Hector but asks. Now, is there anything any of you wish to add?

Moon Elder of Earth: Yes, I would say a few words of encouragement…. Hector, remember that it was the knight of the Round Table who brought back the Grail to Arthur; it is the knight alone on the chess-board that can move in unexpected ways and leap over obstacles. Karen is correct about multi-levelled fields of play, but it goes further even than that because multi-levelledness suggests that there are certain rules and limits. But in the near future, the very thing that will weaken and collapse are these 'rules and limits'. Boundaries will become less defined and anarchy will be very much more dominant. It is only the knights of Truth who can bring about the balance in the midst of chaos. It will be the knights who will be defending the strongholds of the great hierarchy of Compassion who are aiding the Earth whilst it undergoes transformation. But during this time of the Dark of the moon, it is the knights that burn with that light so brilliant, and so will be ever the hope of the New Earth. Peace be upon you friend!

Bhatahivate   25.11.1992

What Heaven's really like- by a leading Brain Surgeon who says he's been there

Read his testimony before you scoff. It might just shake your beliefs.

by Dr. Eben Alexander

When I was a small boy, I was adopted. I grew up remembering nothing of my birth family and unaware that I had a biological sister, named Betsy. Many years later, I went in search of my biological family, but for Betsy it was too late: she had died.

This is the story of how I was reunited with her - in Heaven.

Before I start, I should explain that I am a scientist who has spent a lifetime studying the workings of the brain. My adoptive Father was a neurosurgeon and I followed his path, becoming a neurosurgeon myself who taught brain science at Harvard Medical School.

Although nominally a Christian, I was sceptical when patients described spiritual experiences to me. My knowledge of the brain made me quite sure that out-of-body experiences, angelic encounters and the like were hallucinations, brought on when the brain suffered a trauma.

And then, in the most dramatic circumstances possible, I discovered proof that I was wrong.

Six years ago, I woke up with a searing headache. Within a few hours, I went into a coma: my neocortex, the part of the brain that handles all the thought processes making us human had shut down completely.

At the time, I was working at Lynchburg General Hospital in Virginia, and I was rushed to the emergency room there. The doctors ascertained that I had contracted meningitis - a rare bacterial strain of E coli was in my spinal fluid and eating into my brain like acid. My survival chances were near zero. I was in a deep coma, a vegetative state, and all the higher functions of my brain were offline. Scans showed no conscious activity whatsoever - my brain was not malfunctioning, it was completely unplugged. But my inner self still existed, in defiance of all the known laws of science.

For seven days, as I lay in that unresponsive coma, my consciousness went on a voyage through a series of realms, each one more extraordinary than the last - a journey beyond the physical world and one that, until then, I would certainly have dismissed as impossible.

For thousands of years, ordinary people as well as shamans and mystics have described brief, wonderful glimpses of ethereal realms. I'm not the first person to have discovered that consciousness exists beyond the body.

What is unique in my case is that I am, so far as scientific records show, the only person to have travelled my journey to this heavenly dimension with the cortex in complete shut-down, while under minute observation throughout.

There are medical records for every minute of my coma, and none of them show any indication of brain activity. In other words, as far as neuro-science can say, my journey was not something happening inside my head. Plenty of scientists have a lot of difficulty with this statement. My experience undermines their whole belief system. But the one place I have found ready acceptance is in church, where my story often tallies with people's expectations.

Even the deep notes of the church organ and the glorious colours of the stained glass seem to echo faintly the sights and sounds of Heaven.

Here, then is what I experienced: My Map of Heaven.

After the blinding headache, when I had slipped into the coma, I gradually became aware of being in a primitive, primordial state that felt like being buried in earth. It was, however, not ordinary earth, for all around me I sensed, and sometimes heard and saw, other entities. It was partly horrific, partly comforting and familiar: I felt I had always been part of this primal murk. I am often asked, 'Was this hell?' but I don't think this was - I would expect hell to be at least a little bit interactive, and this was a completely passive experience. I had forgotten what is was to be human, but one important part of my personality was still hard at work: I had a sense of curiosity. I would ask, 'Who, What, Where?' and there was never a flicker of response. After an expanse of time had passed, though I can't begin to guess how long, a light came slowly down from above, throwing off marvellous filaments of living silver and golden effulgence. It was a circular entity, emitting a beautiful, heavenly music that I called the 'Spinning Melody'. The light opened up like a rip in the fabric of that coarse realm, and I felt myself going through the rip, up into a valley full of lush fertile greenery, where waterfalls flowed into crystal pools. There were clouds, like marshmallow puffs of pink and white. Behind them, the sky was a rich blue-black. This world was not vague. It was deeply piercingly alive, and as vivid as the aroma of fried chicken, dazzling as the sunlight off the metalwork of a car, and as startling as the impact of first love.

I know perfectly well how crazy my account sounds, and I sympathise with those who cannot accept it. Like a lot of things in life, it sounds pretty far-fetched till you experience it yourself. There were trees, fields, animals and people. There was water, too, flowing in rivers or descending as rain. Mists rose from the pulsing surfaces of these waters, and fish glided beneath them. Like the earth, the water was deeply familiar. It was as though all the most beautiful waterscapes I ever saw on earth had been beautiful precisely because they were reminding me of this living water. My gaze wanted to travel into it, deeper and deeper. This water seemed higher, and more pure than anything I had experienced before, as if it was somehow closer to the original source. I had stood and admired oceans and rivers across America, from Carolina beaches to west coast streams, but suddenly they all seemed to be lesser versions, little brothers and sisters of this living water.

Nothing is isolated in Heaven. Nothing is alienated. Nothing is disconnected. Everything is one.

I found myself as a speck of awareness on a butterfly wing, amongst pulsing swarms of millions of other butterflies. I witnessed stunning blue-black velvety skies filled with swooping orbs of golden light, angelic choirs leaving trails against the billowing clouds. Those choirs produced hymns and anthems far beyond anything I had encountered on earth. The sound was colossal: an echoing chant that seemed to soak me without making me wet. All my senses had blended. Seeing and hearing were not separate functions. It was as if I could hear the grace and elegance of the airborne creatures, and see the spectacular music that burst out of them. Even before I began to wonder who or what they were, I understood that they made music because they could not contain it. It was the sound of sheer joy. They could no more hold it in as if you could fill your lungs and never breathe out. Simply to experience the music was to join in with it. That was the oneness of Heaven - to hear a sound was to be part of it. Everything was connected to everything else, like the infinitely complex swirls on a Persian carpet or a butterfly's wing. And I was flying on that carpet, riding on that wing. Above the sky, there was a vast array of larger universes that I came to call an 'over-sphere', and I ascended until I reached the Core, that deepest sanctuary of the Divine - infinite inky blackness, filled to overflowing with indescribable, unconditional love. There I encountered the infinitely powerful, all-knowing deity whom I later called Om, because of the sound that vibrated through that realm. I learned lessons there of a depth and beauty entirely beyond my capacity to explain. During this voyage I had a guide. She was an extraordinarily beautiful woman who first appeared as I rode, as the speck of awareness, on the wing of a butterfly. I'd never seen this woman before. I didn't know who she was. Yet her presence was enough to heal my heart, to make me whole in a way I'd never known was possible. Her face was unforgettable. Her eyes were deep blue, and her cheekbones were high. Her face was surrounded by a frame of honey-brown hair. She wore a smock, like a peasant's, woven from sheer colour - indigo, powder-blue and pastel shades of orange and peach. When she looked at me, I felt such an abundance of emotion that, if nothing good had never happened to me before, the whole of my life would have been worth living for that expression in her eyes alone. I was an <u>irreplaceable part of the whole (like all of us), and all the sadness and fear I had ever suffered was a result of my somehow having forgotten this most central of facts.</u> Her message went through me like a breath of wind. It's hard to put it into words, but the essence was this: 'You are loved and cherished, you have nothing to fear. There is nothing you can do wrong'.

I had been in a coma for seven days and showing no improvement. The doctors were just deciding whether to continue with life support, when I suddenly regained consciousness. My eyes just popped open, and I was back. I had no memories of my earthly life, but knew full well where I had been. I had to relearn everything: who, what and where I was. Over days, then weeks, like a gently falling snow, my old, earthly knowledge came back. Words and language returned within hours and days. With the love and gentle coaxing of my family and friends, other memories emerged. By eight weeks, my prior knowledge of science, including the experiences and learning from more than two decades spent as a neurosurgeon in teaching hospitals, returned completely. That full recovery remains a miracle without any explanation from modern medicine.

But I was a different person from the one I had been. The things I had seen and experienced while gone from my body did not fade away, as dreams and hallucinations do. They stayed.

Above all, that image of the woman on the butterfly wing haunted me. And then four months after coming out of my coma, I received a picture in the mail. As a result of my earlier investigations to make contact with my biological family, a relative had sent me a photograph of my sister Betsy - the sister I'd never known. The shock of recognition was total. This was the face of the woman on the butterfly wing. The moment I realised this, something crystallised inside me. That photo was the confirmation that I'd needed. This was proof beyond reproach, of objective reality of my experience. From then on, I was back in the old earthly world I'd left behind before my coma struck, but as a genuinely new person. I had been reborn.

And as I shall reveal on Monday, I am not the only one to have glimpsed the after life - and the wonders it holds.

live music daily

LITTLE INDIA

wide range of quality stalls

lively & creative atmosphere

free workshops & discussions

relaxing & therapeutic

Health & Harmony Festival Weekends

Tapeley Park, Instow, Bideford

weekends of Fun, Healing and Laughter
in Magical Surroundings
wide range of Holistic Therapies on offer
(price capped at only £7 per session)

for further details call Ian on 08453 458 627
e-mail: healthandharmony@thepurplebus.com

May 26/27
June 30/1st July
July 28/29
Aug 25/26

Open 10am - 6pm
Adults £4 - Kids £2
(10% goes to local charity)

www.stonefree.org - design & imaging - 07817 205529
(printed on environmentally friendly paper, of course.)

NO TO GM CAMPAIGN

For many years here at Tapeley Park we have been working with organisations such as Friends of the Earth, Corporate Watch, Genewatch, Farmers for Action, Genetic Engineering Network and Genetic Food Alert, to keep GM crops out of our country and to stop the import of contaminated GM animal feed from the US and Canada especially. It seems as though GM crops will be allowed in through the back door as from 2010. The following article is being submitted to Farmers Weekly on request, which summarises the up-to-date situation:

What will be the consequences for all of us living and working in the countryside, and the consumer, if, as expected, farmers are given the green light to grow GM crops commercially from 2009 onwards?

Biotech crops, according to their producers and many scientists, are the future of farming, improving agriculture, human health, the environment, and the farmer's bank balance – all at the same time. This seems to me to be the premise on which GM crops are sold to farmers by the likes of Monsanto, Syngenta and Bayer. The crops, being genetically modified to withstand powerful systemic sprays such as roundup which pretty much keeps fields free from weeds for months, and inserted with genes which act as pesticides against specific insects thus sometimes doing away with the need to spray altogether, and all the above boxes are surely ticked – or are they?

Certainly in the US and Canada, where farmers were just as hard up as we are in this country now, it made a considerable difference when GM crops were introduced at the start in the 1990's. Many farmers had had to get other jobs to keep them afloat and it paid well for some of them to pay somebody or get in a contractor to give their crops just one spray of roundup, for example, during the growing season and they could sell the product for a decent profit once harvested. Monsanto didn't mention the spring 'clean' and autumn 'clean' of roundup. Most US and Canadian farmers work on minimum till so this is normally necessary. However, to be fair, with the common practice of ploughing in the UK, this would not be so necessary over here if we were to grow GM crops. Add to this, US farmers, especially, with their primarily two crop rotation of Maize and Soya which meant resistance of the weeds built up quite quickly which now necessitates the need for a more toxic cocktail in the tank mix of roundup, 2-4D, atrazine and/or glufosinate ammonium, and with our general 4-year rotation with GM-free wheat and barley, and this 'might' not be such an issue here. In the light of this why are so many of us making such a fuss?

Setting aside the possible benefits in developing countries from growing GM crops that can withstand a degree of salination, and rice with Vitamin A inserted to assist in redu Setting aside the possible benefits in developing countries from growing GM crops that can withstand a degree of salination, and rice with Vitamin A inserted to assist in reducing blindness (both of which are questionable and not relevant to us), and as the 'experiment' has unfolded a number of other issues have arisen shedding a new light on this technology. These include concerns about cross-contamination; possible risk to human health; the long-term effects on both the countryside and us; insurance; the fact that most of the population would rather not eat it; more and more countries refusing to import the stuff; the effect on land values; and concerns about our food chain being controlled from seed to dinner plate by a few very large solely profit driven multinational corporations.

It took just 7 years in Canada to get to the stage that it's now impossible to grow a crop of GM-free Canola (0il seed rape – OSR) due to volunteers and wind-pollen drift. It would, you'd have thought, take much less time on a tiny island like ours. Current separation distances, as stated by DEFRA, between a GM crop and conventional crops stands at 35 meters. In the States the separation distance of GM maize to forage maize and sweetcorn are set at 80m and 200 meters respectively. However, cross-fertilisation has taken place at far greater distances then this. Cross fertilisation between yellow maize and 'blue maize' in the

States demonstrates the problem better than anything else because you can 'see' the results.

One typical example of this in the US is when a Victor Shrock decided to grow blue maize on his 1,600 acres organic farm in 2003. Farmers with holdings 3 miles away complained that their yellow maize had been cross-pollinated with his blue maize. The farmers were not sharing machinery and so on, the seed of Mr. Shrock's neighbours had not been contaminated and the nearest other farm growing blue maize (a rarely grown crop) was 150 miles away. Michael Hart, of Small Family Farm Alliance, stayed with farmers in the US and Canada for some time. He witnessed this phenomena of contamination of yellow maize by blue maize of around 20% when crops were grown 250 meters apart and not even downwind of the 'blue maize'.

On a more serious note we have the discovery that GM Starlink corn has been found in brands of taco shells and chips. Starlink was only approved by US regulators for livestock feed in 1998, after scientists were unable to determine if the gene-spliced maize might cause humans to develop rashes, diarrhoea, and respiratory or other allergic reactions (an all too familiar concern resulting from GM technology). It was NOT approved for human consumption and because of the (unavoidable) cross-contamination (birds and bees can of course carry pollen phenomenal distances), US maize exports to big buyers like Japan and South Korea have been damaged.

We hear some farmers say, " I want to be able to grow what I like," which sounds perfectly reasonable on the surface. However, if say 1% of farmers choose to grow GM crops and contaminate the farms of 99% of the farmers who, say, choose to keep farming conventionally or organically, then surely this is depriving the majority of their rights of choice which to me would seem an act of utter selfishness.

Some farmers might feel that a small degree of contamination is 'no big deal', especially when a GM-free status can still be preserved at levels of less than 9% - which I personally believe to be wrong. 'GM Free' ought to mean what it says. We wouldn't accept antibiotic or BSE "Free" if there was any trace of either in our food. Again I hear a few voices saying antibiotics and BSE are proven to cause ill health, whereas there is no proof GM harms humans. Leaving Genetically Engineered Recumbent Bovine Growth hormone, injected into cows in the States increasing the risk of breast and prostate cancers, aside, and the appalling Truth is that there have been no long-term, peer reviewed, INDEPENDENT studies done on the effect on humans who eat food containing GM crops and products from animals fed GM.

The odd test that has been done independently, have thrown up potentially worrying results. For example, ex-environment Minister Michael Meacher MP, stated in the Guardian on 23.6.03 that the only GM trial done on humans (at Newcastle University)) found that "the GM DNA had been transferred to bacteria in the gut, an alarming find that should be checked and re-checked (to shed light on human health implications)." Likewise, the well-known vilification of Dr Apad Puztai who was sponsored by the Government to carry out safety checks on rats fed GM potatoes. On expressing alarm at his findings, he was hounded out of his job. He clearly felt he found something, so to reassure the public, why didn't the Government commission other scientists do more tests? Instead they've now handed the regulation/safety checks over to the companies who produce GM products and therefore directly stand to profit from as little bad press as possible. Worse still, they don't even have to declare their findings under the legal guise of COMMERCIAL CONFIDENTIALITIY.

The odd time campaign groups HAVE managed to prise out test results, they have uncovered concerns. For example, MON 863 maize was given the commercial green light in July 2006. Greenpeace in Germany managed to unearth the test results and found this GM maize had harmful effects on the kidneys of rats and levels of white blood cells. Even so it is still going into our food chain and we wonder why consumers overwhelmingly would rather not eat the stuff?

A Mori poll published in June showed 61% of people in the UK do not want to eat GM food ingredients. This figure is up by 8% from January 1998 and could rise still further on a crescendo of public debate. Likewise, the figure opposed to

GM taken at the GM Nation debate in 2003 stood at 86%. The 6 meetings were barely publicised (presumably to push through legislation as quickly and quietly as possible), which is why nobody turned up for the first one at the NEC in Birmingham. However, once word got out the other 5 which took place in out of the way locations were packed with those concerned about GM – hence the figure of 86%. This time around, supporters and concerned members of the public were simply told to write to DEFRA HQ in London to express their views. It seems their minds have already been made up, and from 2009 onwards it will be down to us farmers whether we decide to grow GM crops or not.

My point is that the customers don't want it. You just have to click on to the Tesco, Sainsburys (and the rest) websites to see how they promote the fact their own brand products are GM-free. I recently received a letter from Justin King (Sainsbury's) who's at pains to state in his first sentence that; "Following customer demand we were the first major retailer to remove GM ingredients from all our own-brand foods." He goes on to say how they've tried to "move to a non-GM animal feed supply," but this had proven difficult because Gm and non-GM soya and maize are mixed together in silos in the US and Canada. Also Tesco and Sainsbury's, especially, are seeking contracts with suppliers who can guarantee GM-free food. They would not be doing this were it not for the continued rejection of GM by the customers. No other kind of business would be able to produce a product that the vast majority doesn't want more of, the CAP will mean that farm gate prices will be much more dependent on market demand for agricultural products. It will no longer be financially so attractive to sell products that the market does not want into intervention storage in the hope that the EU will release them onto world markets later, courtesy of generous export subsidies.

Last, but not least, how might GM affect our land values? It must be stressed that once GM has been sown, the farm, due to the voracity of the GM gene, will be 'contaminated' (for want of a better word) for many years and possibly for life. Volunteer seeds persist for a long time in the soil. OSR seed has been known to survive for 7 years in reasonable numbers. Just 2 plants/sq m2 gives rise to 3% contamination which takes the crop above the 9% limit currently in place.

There are all sorts of figures currently brandished around in the US claiming big falls in land values on those farms where GM crops have been grown, but no matter, it's not hard to see that if you're a farmer who has grown GM you will have to keep growing it. Converting to becoming organic, which is becoming ever more popular and where premium prices will only increase, will be nigh on impossible with obvious repercussions on land values. The concern is that even if you are an organic farmer, or a conventional one for that matter, and a farmer is growing GM crops nearby, you could lose your organic status at the drop of a hat with the knock-on-effect on the capital value of your Holding.

This has recently happened to organic growers in Spain when traces of GM were found in their maize and sweetcorn resulting from cross-pollination from a nearby farm. The devastating result was they lost their organic status on EVERYTHING. Is it any wonder that the NFU Mutual places the insurance of GM in the same category as asbestos and terrorism?

If any farmer thinks he will be able to dip in and out of growing GM and non-GM crops, he should read 'Monsanto versus US Farmers' written by the Food Safety Centre – an independent agricultural body in the States. A list as long as the River Nile (well not quite), has been compiled of those farmers who have been forced by Monsanto, who have used the legal system wherever necessary, to keep growing GM crops.

The RICS has been lobbying Parliament to make a Public Register of farms growing GM crops. This is, after all, an EU Directive and thus Law. It is surely a right for anybody buying land to know its history. However, DEFRA has overruled the EU and deemed this unnecessary. It did the same during Foot and Mouth (when it was called MAFF), and thereby pitted farmer against farmer – as many of us remember only too well and with a lot of pain. I can't begin to imagine how much worse this will be when GM is given the go ahead. The Biotech companies have already absolved themselves from any responsibility once the seed is sold so it will be us against our neighbour. How things currently stand is under something called the SCIMAC protocol which 'requires' GM growers to liase with neighbours regarding their planting intentions. However, the SCIMAC code is a voluntary protocol which cannot be enforced through the Courts and cannot therefore be relied upon by neighbouring farmers. This could mean that many of us will be in for a nasty shock when our crops are tested.

To sum up: Do we in the countryside want to give up control of our choices and businesses to a few ruthless, solely profit driven large corporations (see attached Technology Agreement setting out Terms and Conditions for further verification). We are an island, and as such have the most fantastic opportunity to be a source of GM-free food, plus we have a potentially invaluable GM-free seed bank for ourselves and the world in the future. This is provided we can ALL resist the temptation of short-term profits. In the US and Canada, many farmers were given (bribed in my view) their seed for free for the first 2 to 3 years by Monsanto. According to Michael Hart, many now seriously regret their decision. Nobody knows, after all, where we might be with crop mutations say 20 generations down the line. As such I implore farmers to write to Mr. Milliband at DEFRA, Noble House, 17 Smith Square, London. SW1 P3JR to beg him to keep us GM FREE.

I will leave you with the most surreal, crazy moment of all which puts all else in the "second tier" category.

Jarrick and Betina were odd …… very odd and poor, Roger was terrified of accidently crossing her severe path resulting in a "dressing down". Roger was on his way to bed when he heard shuffling sounds and strange noises emanating from the small airing cupboard on the middle floor.

Exasperated that the hippie had "forgotten" to shut the cupboards and turn the light off yet again, Roger flung open the cupboard full of linen, etc only to expose Betina kneeling in front of Jarrick, to which Jarrick said …… "and this is where we keep the hoovers".

Printed in Great Britain
by Amazon

32839265R00112